SABBATH Dinner COOKBOOK

Favorite vegetarian meal ideas for celebrating Sabbath with family and friends

JACQUELYN FAUCHER BECK
JEANNE BECK JARNES
KRISTEN JARNES

Pacific Press® Publishing Association
Nampa, Idaho
Oshawa, Ontario, Canada

Edited by: Aileen Andres Sox
Cover art colorization, cover and inside design: Michelle C. Petz

INTRODUCTION

Traditionally, Sabbath dinner has been the time when friends and family get together to enjoy each other's company. After all, you have to cook anyway—why not make just a little more and invite someone to share it with you? It's a great time to ask that new family over, or those two elderly widows who sit together in church every Sabbath, or that single person who may feel out of place in our "family oriented" social circles. Sabbath is the perfect opportunity to put your gift of hospitality to work!

Sometimes, the most difficult part of all is deciding what to make for Sabbath dinner. Well, wonder no longer. If you have this book in your hands, you are holding 40 menus from some of the best cooks we know! They range from simple Sabbath agape meals of soup, salad, and bread to more extravagant, festive meals that feed a crowd.

Some menus will require advance preparation; some can be prepared once you get home from church. We prefer to do as much as possible ahead of time so that it doesn't take long to get the meal on the table. Setting the table Friday night, or before leaving for church Sabbath morning, helps to provide a relaxed atmosphere when your guests arrive. (If nothing else, it makes you look organized!)

Because Sabbath dinners are often "company food," they tend to be more caloric than what we usually eat. To balance a high caloric entrée, include a wide variety of fresh and cooked vegetables in your menu. We have provided the nutritional information for most of the recipes in this book. However, there are many ways to cut additional fats and calories, and you can find a thorough discussion of this on pages 156, 157 in the first book of this series, Adventist Potluck Cookbook. (Nutritional analysis was calculated with Nutritionalist Five and Master Cook software programs. Results may very depending on product used.)

Thank you to everyone who took the time to share favorite menus for this cookbook and to Frank Kravig for helping us calculate the nutritional analysis. Special thanks to Laurie Jarnes Brown, Gayle Beck, Vicki Jarnes, Kathy Miller, Van Haas, June Pfaff, and Edna Abrams, the cooks who so willingly prepared many of the recipes for our "tasting parties." Thank you also to our daddies, spouses, cousins, and friends, the enthusiastic guinea pigs who sampled dish after dish. We have had fun, and the memories we've made are priceless.

Here's to many wonderful Sabbath dinners around your table!

"True intimacy flourish(es) at tables. . . . At the table you have the best eye contact. . . . People push their empty plates to one side and linger longer and longer at the table. A table is the most beautiful piece of furniture there is."

–Reader's Digest, October, 2000, page 125.

SABBATH DINNER MENU #1

Contributed by Jackie Beck
College Place, Washington

Jackie says: Chicken Pot Pie was one of the first vegetarian recipes I learned 52 years ago as a new bride in Texas. It was a favorite with my children and is now with the grandchildren. Everybody expects it at least once when we're all together! I prepare it on Friday, cover and refrigerate. On Sabbath morning, I put it uncovered in the oven and set the timer so it will be done about the time we return home from church. It needs to sit about ten minutes before serving.

Chicken Pot Pie

Green beans with slivered almonds

Crookneck Squash

Tossed salad

Dinner rolls

Angel Food Cake With Raspberries

Filtered Water with
   Sliced Lemons and Limes

Chicken Pot Pie

serves 8

1 20-ounce can Worthington® *Low Fat Vegetable Skallops*® (reserve broth)
1 12-ounce can nonfat evaporated milk
1/3 cup finely chopped onion
1/4 cup + 2 teaspoons olive oil
3 hard-boiled eggs, peeled and diced
1/2 cup Morningstar Farms® *Scramblers*®
6 heaping tablespoons flour
1 tablespoon seasoned salt
Pastry pie crust for one pie

In two-quart measuring cup, mix the *Skallops*® broth and evaporated milk. Add enough water to make 5 cups. *The broth is one of the secrets of this dish, so be sure and use it!* Set aside. Slice *Skallops*® crosswise into 1/2-inch slices. Heat 1/4 cup oil in large skillet. Add onions and sauté until tender. Carefully remove onions and add *Skallops*® to the oil. Allow *Skallops*® to fry on medium heat for about 5 minutes before turning or stirring so that one side becomes medium brown. Turn and fry briefly on the other side. Remove from oil and add to the onions.

To make the pot pie gravy, first remove skillet from heat. Add the extra 2 teaspoons of oil. Pour the *Scramblers*® into the skillet, beating with a fork to blend thoroughly with the oil. Return to heat. As the *Scramblers*® begin to cook, keep mashing with the fork so they break into fine pieces and begin to brown. When the oil bubbles up around the *Scramblers*®, add the flour and continue stirring until the flour is well browned. Remove from heat and pour the *Skallops*® broth, milk, and

PER SERVING

Calories:	*279*
Total Fat:	*15g*
Cholesterol:	*65mg*
Sodium:	*902mg*
Carbs:	*19g*
Protein:	*17g*

water mixture into the egg-flour blend all at once. Stir briskly and return to heat. Stir until gravy thickens. You may want to add a bit more water. The gravy should not be too thick, as it thickens somewhat while baking. Add seasoning salt to taste.

Add hard-boiled eggs to the gravy, along with the fried *Skallops*® and onions. Mix well and pour into a 9" x 13" casserole, greased lightly with cooking spray. Roll pastry to pie crust thickness. Using a glass or biscuit cutter dipped into flour, cut pie dough into circles and arrange on top of the pot pie. Bake at 350°F for 30 to 45 minutes, or until pie is hot and bubbly and crust is slightly browned. Let set 10 minutes before serving.

Crookneck Squash

1 tablespoon olive oil
2 to 3 cloves of garlic, minced
6 to 8 yellow crookneck squash, sliced into 1/2-inch slices

Sauté the garlic in olive oil for about 20 to 30 seconds, then add the sliced squash and about 1/2 cup water. Bring to a boil and simmer for about 5 minutes, or until squash is just tender. Add salt to taste and serve immediately.

PER SERVING	
Calories:	38
Total Fat:	2g
Cholesterol:	0mg
Sodium:	2mg
Carbs:	5g
Protein:	1g

Angel Food Cake With Raspberries

serves 10

2 10-ounce packages frozen raspberries,
    thawed and drained (reserve juice)
2 tablespoons cornstarch
Sugar to taste
Prepared angel food cake
1 8-ounce container light whipped topping

PER SERVING

Calories:	*203*
Total Fat:	*3g*
Cholesterol:	*0mg*
Sodium:	*255mg*
Carbs:	*41g*
Protein:	*2g*

In a medium saucepan, combine berry juice and cornstarch. Bring to a boil and stir until slightly thickened. Add berries and sugar to taste. *If you make this raspberry topping while you are preparing the meal, it will be the right temperature to serve at the end of the meal.*

Place cake slices on individual dessert plates. Spoon raspberry topping on each slice, add whipped topping, and garnish with a maraschino cherry, if desired.

Filtered Water With Sliced Lemons and Limes

My friend, Diane Matson, shared this attractive way to serve water as a beverage. Thinly slice 1 or 2 limes and 1 or 2 lemons. Place approximately 4 slices of each in a pretty glass pitcher along with some ice cubes and fill with water. Slit one side of remaining slices, slipping one slice onto the rim of each glass for a festive look!

SABBATH DINNER MENU #2

Contributed by Jeanne Jarnes
Caldwell, Idaho

Jeanne says: Wait until you taste this Eggplant Parmesan! It absolutely melts in your mouth. And, amazingly, you don't need a bit of oil to prepare it! I often use tofu mozzarella cheese and leave off the Parmesan cheese, which makes it nondairy too. Sometimes, instead of the potatoes and broccoli in this menu, I cook angel hair pasta and toss it with crispy-tender broccoli and cauliflower that have been stir-fried in a little olive oil and fresh garlic. Serve in a big pasta bowl, sprinkled with toasted pine nuts.

When I make a tossed salad, I like to use a variety of veggies. I start with crispy dark green Romaine lettuce leaves and add a selection of colored peppers, radishes, red cabbage, English cucumber, broccoli and cauliflower flowerets, green onions, celery—and even zucchini! Since I like fresh lemon juice on my own salad, I include a small bowl of lemon wedges on the table, along with the regular salad dressing for my guests. I generally serve the feta cheese in a separate bowl for guests to add to their salad if they wish—and don't forget the seasoned croutons!

Eggplant Parmesan

Quick and Crunchy
Garlic Baked Potatoes

Steamed broccoli
(or other green vegetable)

Tossed salad with feta cheese

Whole wheat rolls

Brownies topped with chocolate
chip mint ice cream and
fudge sauce

Eggplant Parmesan

serves 8

1/3 cup seasoned Italian breadcrumbs
3/4 teaspoon oregano leaves
3 tablespoons light mayonnaise
2 or 3 small eggplants (about 1 pound each),
    cut crosswise into 3/4-inch-thick slices
1 26-ounce jar spaghetti sauce
2 cups shredded mozzarella cheese
2 tablespoons grated Parmesan cheese

PER SERVING	
Calories:	203
Total Fat:	8g
Cholesterol:	19mg
Sodium:	712mg
Carbs:	25g
Protein:	11g

On waxed paper, combine breadcrumbs and oregano. Lightly brush eggplant slices on one side with mayonnaise, and coat on same side with crumb mixture. In 9" x 13" baking dish, arrange eggplant slices, crumb sides up, overlapping slices if necessary. Cover with waxed paper and cook in microwave on high for 12 to 15 minutes until eggplant is very tender. Rotate dish halfway through cooking. Sprinkle 1 1/2 cups mozzarella cheese over eggplant. Spoon spaghetti sauce over all, then top with remaining mozzarella and Parmesan cheese. *If you are preparing this just in time to eat, warm the sauce before spooning it over the eggplant, top with cheese and microwave for another 4 minutes. If you are preparing this ahead of time, you don't need to heat the sauce first. When you get home from church, just pop the dish into the oven and let it heat up while you prepare the rest of the meal.*

Quick and Crunchy Garlic Baked Potatoes

serves 8

4 or 5 large baking potatoes
Garlic powder and salt
2 tablespoons olive oil

Cut potatoes in half lengthwise. Sprinkle each cut side with garlic powder and salt. Measure olive oil into jellyroll pan or glass baking dish. Place potatoes, cut side down, in pan, making sure cut sides are coated with oil. Bake at 375° to 400°F for 30 minutes or until tender and crunchy on the cut side. *I usually put these in the oven and set the automatic timer before leaving for church. This gives them plenty of time to bake well and form a nice crunchy crust.*

Cheesy Lentil Soup

Garlic Bread

Tossed salad

Rae's Peach and Berry Cobbler

SABBATH DINNER MENU #3

Contributed by Kristen Jarnes
Spokane, Washington

Kristi says: This soup was actually a winter Friday night tradition in our house when my brother, Todd, and I were growing up. When I got my own place in college, I would invite my friends over for "soup night" after a hard week of studying. Todd's friends in the dorm would beg to come along with him when they knew lentil soup was on. Those evenings are some of my favorite college memories. I even took the herbs with me to Ukraine when I spent a year as a missionary there. Whether I'm making it for supper or for dinner on Sabbath, the smell of this soup cooking on Friday afternoon makes any place feel like home to me.

Cheesy Lentil Soup

serves 10

2 cups lentils
10 cups water
4 teaspoons salt
1/2 teaspoon thyme
1/2 teaspoon marjoram
1/3 cup olive oil

2 large onions, sliced
2 large carrots, sliced
1/3 cup dried parsley
1 quart tomatoes
1 cup grated cheddar cheese (optional)

PER SERVING

Calories:	259
Total Fat:	11g
Cholesterol:	0mg
Sodium:	858mg
Carbs:	30g
Protein:	12g

Wash lentils and put in large kettle with water and herbs (except parsley). Bring to a boil. Cover and simmer for 15 minutes.

While lentils are simmering, slice onions and carrots. Heat olive oil in large frying pan. Sauté onions and carrots until tender. Add onions, carrots, parsley, and tomatoes to the lentils. Simmer at least 1 or 2 hours until lentils are tender. (Can simmer for several hours.) If desired, put 1 to 2 tablespoons grated cheese in each bowl before filling with soup.

Garlic Bread

I usually use my grandma's recipe (see p. 22) with some changes. I use French or Italian bread and substitute parsley for the dill. *Tip for the uncouth:* this garlic bread is delicious dipped into the soup. . . .

Rae's Peach and Berry Cobbler

serves 8

Filling:
1 tablespoon cornstarch
1/4 cup brown sugar
1/2 cup cold water
2 cups sliced fresh peaches, sweetened
1 cup fresh blueberries
1 tablespoon + 1/4 cup butter or
    margarine, divided
1 tablespoon lemon juice

Topping:
1 cup sifted enriched flour
1/2 cup + 2 tablespoons
    granulated sugar, divided
1 1/2 teaspoon baking powder
1/2 teaspoon salt
1/2 cup 2% milk
1/4 teaspoon nutmeg

Mix first three FILLING ingredients in a medium saucepan. Add fruits. Cook and stir until mixture thickens. Add 1 tablespoon butter and lemon juice. Pour into 8-inch round ovenware cake pan or 9" x 13" baking dish.

To make TOPPING, sift flour, 1/2 cup granulated sugar, baking powder, and salt together in a large mixing bowl. Add milk and 1/4 cup softened butter or margarine all at once. Beat until smooth. Spread over fruit. Sprinkle with 2 tablespoons sugar and 1/4 teaspoon nutmeg. Bake at 350°F for 30 minutes or until done. Serve warm with cream or vanilla ice cream.

Note: You can use canned or frozen fruit. Drain canned fruit, retaining 1/2 cup syrup to use in place of water.

PER SERVING

Calories:	281
Total Fat:	8g
Cholesterol:	22mg
Sodium:	312mg
Carbs:	51g
Protein:	3g

Sabbath Dinner Menu #4

Contributed by Rena Glubay
Boise, Idaho

Jeanne says: Rena is kept plenty busy mothering twin boys and holding down a full-time job in the Information Systems Services Department at Pacific Press! She likes to keep her menus simple and healthy.

Rena says: This is my husband's favorite soup. It can be cooked a day before and reheated. The Yogurt Carob Cake is a good one even for people who do not like carob.

Carrot Soup

Salad

Crusty bread with butter

Yogurt Carob Cake

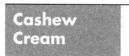

Carrot Soup

serves 6

2 tablespoons uncooked brown rice
2 medium onions, chopped
5 cloves garlic, chopped
6 medium carrots, sliced
4 cups vegetable broth

1/2 teaspoon salt
1/4 teaspoon dried thyme leaves
1/8 teaspoon chili powder
1/8 teaspoon curry powder
1/2 cup Cashew Cream (recipe follows)

In 3-quart saucepan, simmer rice, onions, and garlic in vegetable broth, covered, for 30 minutes. Add remaining ingredients (except cashew cream); bring to a boil. Reduce heat to low and simmer, uncovered, 30 minutes or until carrots are tender. Cool slightly.

In a blender, purée small batches of the soup at high speed until smooth. Pour puréed mixture back into saucepan. Gradually stir in Cashew Cream. Over low heat, cook 3 minutes until heated through. Serve with salad and crusty bread with butter.

PER SERVING	
Calories:	*106*
Total Fat:	*4g*
Cholesterol:	*0mg*
Sodium:	*886mg*
Carbs:	*17g*
Protein:	*4g*

Cashew Cream

1/4 cup cashews
1/2 cup water

Process in blender at medium to high speed until smooth.

Yogurt Carob Cake

serves 9

2 eggs or 1/2 cup Morningstar Farms® *Scramblers®*
1 1/3 cups firmly packed brown sugar
1 cup plain yogurt
1 teaspoon vanilla
1 teaspoon maple flavoring
1 cup sifted whole-wheat flour
1/3 cup carob powder
1 teaspoon baking soda
1 teaspoon baking powder
1/2 cup carob chips, finely chopped
1/2 cup pecans, finely chopped

PER SERVING	
Calories:	*320*
Total Fat:	*10g*
Cholesterol:	*49mg*
Sodium:	*228mg*
Carbs:	*54g*
Protein:	*7g*

Preheat oven to 350°F. Beat eggs, brown sugar, yogurt, vanilla, and maple flavoring until blended. Combine flour, carob powder, baking soda, and baking powder and gradually add to egg mixture, stirring until moistened. Pour into an 8-inch square pan that has been sprayed with cooking spray and dusted with flour. Mix carob chips and pecans and sprinkle over cake. Bake for 35 minutes. Cool cake on a rack for 20 minutes before slicing.

SABBATH DINNER MENU #5

Contributed by Betsy Matthews
Thousand Oaks, California

Greek Garbanzo Stew

Baked potatoes

Zucchini (or your favorite
    green vegetable)

Cole slaw or garden salad

Rolls

Fruit yogurt with cookies

Betsy says: A college classmate, Marcia King, shared this recipe with me back in the late 1960s. It has been one of our favorites and is an easy Sabbath main dish. It makes a good "make ahead" meal, as it freezes beautifully, and is better if reheated.

Greek Garbanzo Stew

serves 8

PER SERVING

Calories:	*302*
Total Fat:	*16g*
Cholesterol:	*0mg*
Sodium:	*883mg*
Carbs:	*32g*
Protein:	*10g*

3 1-pound cans drained garbanzo beans
1 cup chopped onions
1 teaspoon crushed rosemary (dried may be used, but fresh is better)
3 tablespoons minced parsley
1 28-ounce can tomatoes or 1 quart home-canned tomatoes, mashed
Salt to taste
4 cloves garlic or 1/8 teaspoon garlic powder
1/2 cup olive oil
1 teaspoon seasoned salt

Combine all ingredients in a 2 1/2-quart casserole. Cover and bake at 325°F for two to three hours, or more. *Betsy sometimes puts this in the oven at 250°F to cook overnight. Delicious!*

Mom's Lasagna

Green peas

Greek Tossed Salad
   With Olive Oil Dressing

Sourdough French Bread
   With Garlic Spread

Rose Roger's English Trifle

SABBATH DINNER MENU #6

Contributed by Jackie Beck
College Place, Washington

Jackie says: This lasagna is different, using rotini (spiral pasta) in place of regular lasagna noodles. I make the lasagna on Friday, cover it with foil, and refrigerate. Sabbath morning, I just put it in the oven and set the timer to be done about the time we return from church. I prepare the garlic butter and butter the bread on Friday, wrap in foil and refrigerate. I also make the English Trifle on Friday. Just before serving add sliced bananas and whipped topping and garnish with chopped nuts and maraschino cherries. It looks beautiful and is a dessert you'll be proud to serve!

Mom's Lasagna

serves 8

2 tablespoons olive oil
1 20-ounce can Worthington® *Vegetarian Burger®*
2 medium onions, chopped fine
26 ounces of your favorite prepared spaghetti sauce
1/2 cup imitation bacon bits (optional)
1 3-ounce package light cream cheese
1 cup 2% cottage cheese
1 cup light sour cream
1/3 cup finely sliced green onions,
1 tablespoon finely chopped green pepper
1 12-ounce package rotini or wide egg noodles
1/2 cup cheddar or Parmesan cheese (optional)

Heat oil in large frying pan. Brown 1 can Worthington® *Vegetarian Burger®*, then add chopped onion and fry a bit more until tender. Add spaghetti sauce and bacon bits. Set aside. In a large bowl, mix together softened cream cheese, cottage cheese, and sour cream. Add green onions and green pepper. Mix thoroughly. Set aside. Cook noodles, drain, splash with cold water, and drain again.

Put half the noodles in a well-oiled 9" x 13" casserole. Spread the cream cheese mixture on top of the noodles. Spread the remaining half of the noodles on top of the cream cheese mixture. Spoon the burger mixture across the top of the casserole. Top with some cheddar or Parmesan cheese, if desired. Bake uncovered at 350°F for 45 minutes.

PER SERVING	
Calories:	293
Total Fat:	11g
Cholesterol:	35mg
Sodium:	789mg
Carbs:	27g
Protein:	21g

Greek Tossed Salad

Use the following ingredients to make a tossed salad:

Romaine lettuce, torn into bite-sized pieces
Tomato, cut in wedges
Cucumber, sliced thinly
Red onion, sliced thinly

Black olives, cut in half
Feta cheese, crumbled
Seasoned croutons (optional)

Olive Oil Dressing

serves 8

1/4 cup olive oil
1/3 cup lemon juice
1/8 teaspoon oregano flakes

1 clove garlic, crushed
Salt to taste

Blend all ingredients and pour over the tossed salad just before serving.

Sourdough French Bread With Garlic Spread

1 stick margarine, softened to room temperature
4 cloves garlic, pressed through garlic press
Parmesan cheese

Dill weed
Paprika

Combine margarine and pressed garlic. Spread on the French Bread, which has been split in half, lengthwise. Sprinkle with Parmesan cheese, then dill weed. Sprinkle paprika in diagonal stripes across the bread. Broil in oven at 300°F, until the bread is hot and begins to brown around edges. Cut and serve.

Rose Roger's English Trifle

serves 10

PER SERVING

Calories:	*296*
Total Fat:	*11g*
Cholesterol:	*6mg*
Sodium:	*175mg*
Carbs:	*47g*
Protein:	*3g*

A note from Jackie: I was first introduced to this delicious English trifle when my husband Ed and I were guests in the home of A. George and Rose Rogers in Oshawa, Ontario, Canada. A. George was administrator of Branson Hospital while Ed was chairman of the board. Rose was an accomplished musician and gracious hostess. It is a privilege to share this recipe with you in her memory.

20 snack-size pecan shortbread cookies (approximate)
1/2 cup strawberry jam (approximate)
1 3-ounce box cherry or raspberry gelatin
1 3-ounce box vanilla pudding (cooked version)
1 8-ounce carton light whipped topping
2 bananas
8 maraschino cherries
1/4 cup chopped walnuts or pecans

Spread cookies with jam and place in bottom of glass pedestal bowl (use enough cookies to cover the bottom of the bowl). Make gelatin according to directions and pour over cookies while the gelatin is very hot. Prepare pudding according to package directions and pour hot pudding over the hot gelatin (you will get a ribbon-like effect). Cover with plastic wrap and refrigerate until firm.

Just before serving: Thinly slice two bananas on top of pudding. Spread whipped topping over all and garnish with maraschino cherries and nuts.

Macaroni and Cheese Deluxe

Ginnie's Meatloaf

Green Beans and Baby Carrots
  With Dill Weed

Layered Chicken Salad

Frosted Salad

Crescent rolls

White grape juice

Lemon Pudding Dessert

SABBATH DINNER MENU # 7

Contributed by Ginnie Geary
Calhoun, Georgia

Ginnie says: This dinner is attractive because of the different colors of food on the menu. Meat lovers think the loaf has meat in it and are surprised to find out differently. The Layered Chicken Salad is different because of the pickle relish in it. Serving white grape juice is nice, especially if there are children present—no dark grape juice stains to remove from tablecloth or carpet! Since this is a very satisfying menu, the Lemon Pudding Dessert is jut right—not too heavy, but very tasty.

Jackie says: Ginnie and I first became acquainted in 1973 when people asked Ginnie, who lived in Spokane, Washington, if she had a sister who worked at the Adventist Book Center in Seattle. Later, when Ed and I moved to the Upper Columbia Conference where Ginnie was the receptionist, she asked, "Who is it that works in the ABC in Seattle who looks like me?" I took one look at her and said, "Me." That began our special friendship and we have laughed so many times over the fact that people seem to be confused as to whether they were talking to Ginnie or to me. Our voices even sound alike and we have fooled her husband, Bill, over the phone. Since neither of us has a sister, we have adopted each other. Ginnie loves to cook and entertain and I know you will enjoy her recipes.

Macaroni and Cheese Deluxe

serves 8

PER SERVING

Calories:	*315*
Total Fat:	*14g*
Cholesterol:	*70mg*
Sodium:	*651mg*
Carbs:	*26g*
Protein:	*21g*

1 8-ounce package macaroni
2 cups low fat cottage cheese
8 ounces light sour cream
1 egg, beaten or
    1/4 cup Morningstar Farms® *Scramblers®*
2 cups grated cheddar cheese
3/4 teaspoon salt
Paprika

Cook macaroni according to package directions; drain, rinse, and set aside. Combine other ingredients (except paprika) in a two-quart bowl. Add macaroni and stir well. Spoon into lightly greased two-quart casserole. Sprinkle with paprika. Bake at 350°F for 45 minutes.

Ginnie's Meatloaf

serves 8

1/4 cup butter or margarine
1 medium onion, chopped fine
1/2 green pepper, chopped fine
4 slices whole wheat bread, cubed
4 eggs, beaten or
    1 cup Morningstar Farms® *Scramblers*®
1/2 teaspoon paprika

1 teaspoon garlic powder
1/2 teaspoon poultry seasoning
1 20-ounce can Worthington®
    Vegetarian Burger®
1 cup grated Colby cheese
1/2 cup brown sugar
1/2 cup ketchup

PER SERVING

Calories:	253
Total Fat:	13g
Cholesterol:	97mg
Sodium:	641mg
Carbs:	19g
Protein:	16g

Sauté onion and green pepper in butter or margarine. Stir in the cubed bread and mix well. Beat eggs with paprika, garlic powder, and poultry seasoning. Combine egg mixture with burger and grated cheese. Mix well and combine with onion, green pepper, and bread mix. Stir until well blended. Mix brown sugar and ketchup together. Grease a loaf pan and put half the topping in the bottom of pan. Add loaf mixture, and spread the other half of the topping over the loaf. Bake at 375°F for one hour. Cool 15 minutes before inverting onto plate and slicing. Garnish with parsley sprigs.

Green Beans and Baby Carrots With Dill Weed

Cook fresh green beans and baby carrots together until done. Drain water and add salt and butter as desired. Sprinkle with dill weed.

Layered Chicken Salad

serves 10

2 12.5-ounce cans Worthington®
   FriChik®, diced
2 cups torn lettuce
1 cup cooked long grain rice
1 10-ounce package frozen peas,
   thawed
1/4 cup minced fresh parsley
2 large tomatoes,
   seeded and chopped
1 cup thinly sliced cucumber
1 small sweet red pepper, chopped
1 small green pepper, chopped

Dressing:
1 cup light mayonnaise
1/2 cup light sour cream
1/2 cup finely chopped onion
1/4 cup sweet pickle relish
2 tablespoons 2% milk
1/2 teaspoon celery seed
1/2 teaspoon ground mustard
1/2 teaspoon garlic salt

PER SERVING	
Calories:	273
Total Fat:	17g
Cholesterol:	18mg
Sodium:	627mg
Carbs:	20g
Protein:	12g

In a 3-quart glass bowl, layer 1 can of *Fri-Chik*® and the lettuce. Combine rice, peas, and parsley; spoon over lettuce. Layer with tomatoes, cucumber, peppers, and remaining chicken. Combine DRESSING ingredients; spoon over salad. Cover and refrigerate for 8 hours, or overnight. Toss before serving.

Frosted Salad

serves 9

1 3-ounce package lemon gelatin
1 cup hot water
1 cup cold water
1 8-ounce can crushed pineapple, drained (reserve juice)

Topping:
1 cup pineapple juice (reserved juice + water)
1/2 cup sugar
1 egg, beaten or 1/4 cup Morningstar Farms® *Scramblers*®
2 rounded tablespoons flour
2 tablespoons butter or margarine
1/2 cup cheese, grated
1 cup whipped cream or nondairy light whipped topping

PER SERVING	
Calories:	173
Total Fat:	6g
Cholesterol:	30mg
Sodium:	100mg
Carbs:	26g
Protein:	3g

Prepare gelatin according to directions on package. Add crushed pineapple. Then you may add bananas, mandarin oranges, marshmallows, or whatever you desire. Pour into a 9-inch square pan, cover with plastic wrap and refrigerate until set.

TOPPING: Melt butter; remove from heat. Mix flour and sugar; add to butter. Combine egg and pineapple juice; stir into butter/flour mixture. Return to heat and cook on low, stirring constantly, until thickened. Chill in refrigerator. Fold in 1 cup whipped cream or topping. Spread on top of gelatin mixture and sprinkle with grated cheese. Chill in refrigerator.

Lemon Pudding Dessert

serves 12

1 cup cold butter or margarine
2 cups flour
1 8-ounce package cream cheese, softened
1 cup confectioner's sugar
1 8-ounce carton frozen whipped topping, thawed and divided
3 cups cold milk
2 3.4-ounce packages instant lemon pudding mix

PER SERVING	
Calories:	332
Total Fat:	17g
Cholesterol:	11mg
Sodium:	392mg
Carbs:	39g
Protein:	5g

In a bowl, cut butter or margarine into the flour, until crumbly. Press into an ungreased 9" x 13" baking pan. Bake at 350°F for 18 to 22 minutes, or until set. Cool on a wire rack.

In a mixing bowl, beat cream cheese and sugar until smooth. Fold in 1 cup whipped topping. Spread over crust. Beat milk and pudding mix on low speed for 2 minutes. Carefully spread over the cream cheese layer. Top with the remaining topping. Refrigerate for at least 1 hour.

Noodle Dish

Frozen peas

Orange-Pineapple Gelatin Salad

Relishes

Rolls

Fruit punch

Coffee Cake

S A B B A T H   D I N N E R   M E N U   # 8

Contributed by Debbie Darnall
Mesa, Arizona

Debbie says: This menu takes about 1 1/2 to 2 hours of preparation on Friday. I mix the cake and bake it while I prepare the other food. I prepare the noodle dish and place it in the refrigerator, then mix the gelatin salad and refrigerate it in an airtight container. Finally, I arrange the relishes on a plate and cover them. Sabbath morning, before I leave for church, I put the noodle dish into the oven and set the timer for 45 minutes at 350°F. When I arrive home from church, I warm the rolls in the oven and cook the frozen peas, adding butter and salt just before serving. Last of all, I make the punch by mixing pineapple juice, orange juice, and lemonade.

Noodle Dish

serves 8

2 tablespoons margarine
1 medium onion, chopped fine
1 cup celery, chopped fine
4 4-ounce cans mushrooms
1 13-ounce can Worthington® *Diced Chik*®, drained
1 teaspoon oil
3 eggs or 3/4 cup Morningstar Farms® *Scramblers*®
2 10.75-ounce cans condensed cream of mushroom soup, undiluted
1/8 teaspoon of thyme
1 12-ounce can evaporated milk
1/2 cup brewer's yeast flakes
1 cup noodles, cooked and drained
1 teaspoon salt

PER SERVING	
Calories:	193
Total Fat:	7g
Cholesterol:	10mg
Sodium:	955mg
Carbs:	19g
Protein:	14g

Melt margarine in medium frying pan. Sauté the onion, celery, and mushrooms. After sautéing, put into a mixing bowl. Add drained *Diced Chik*®.

Heat 1 teaspoon oil in frying pan. Soft-scramble 3 eggs. Be sure not to hard cook. Put in bowl with *Diced Chik*® mixture. Add remaining ingredients. Bake in oiled casserole at 350°F for 45 minutes, uncovered; 1 hour if you like the top crunchy.

Orange-Pineapple Gelatin Salad

serves 8

1 6-ounce package orange gelatin
1 14-ounce can crushed pineapple, drained
3 11-ounce cans mandarin oranges
1 cup grated carrots

Mix all ingredients and add to cooled gelatin. Refrigerate in an airtight container.

PER SERVING	
Calories:	*124*
Total Fat:	*.06g*
Cholesterol:	*0mg*
Sodium:	*29mg*
Carbs:	*30g*
Protein:	*1g*

Coffee Cake

serves 8

2 cups flour
1 cup sugar
2 teaspoons baking powder
1/2 cup butter or margarine
1 egg, beaten or
    1/4 cup Morningstar Farms®
    Scramblers®

3/4 cup 2% milk (approximate)
1 30-ounce can cherry pie filling

Crumb topping:
1 cup flour
1/2 cup sugar
1/2 cup butter or margarine

PER SERVING	
Calories:	*438*
Total Fat:	*16g*
Cholesterol:	*19mg*
Sodium:	*270mg*
Carbs:	*69g*
Protein:	*5g*

Mix dry ingredients well, and cut in 1/2 cup margarine. Put egg in measuring cup, fill with milk to one cup, and mix well. Add egg mixture to dry ingredients. Pour into a 9" x 13" greased cake pan. Spread top of cake with a large can of cherry pie filling. Mix CRUMB TOPPING ingredients and sprinkle on top. Bake for 35 minutes at 400°F. Serve warm with a scoop of vanilla ice cream.

SABBATH DINNER MENU #9

Contributed by Ellen Reiner
Fountain Hills, Arizona

Jackie says: Ellen is a fabulous cook and it is always a treat to be invited to her home. When we had our "tasting parties" for this book, her Barbecued Meatballs were a real hit!

Barbecued Meatballs

Ellen's Potato Casserole

Peas With Dill

Carrots With Lemony
    Honey-Mustard Sauce

Cucumber Cream Salad

Garlic Bread With Oregano
    and Parmesan

Fudge Brownie Pie
    With Hot Fudge Sauce

Fizzy Cranberry-Lemonade Punch

Barbecued Meatballs

serves 18 (72 meatballs; 4 per serving)

1 medium onion, chopped fine
1 20-ounce can Worthington® *Vegetarian Burger*®
3 eggs or
    3/4 cup Morningstar Farms® *Scramblers*®
2 cups finely chopped pecans
1 1/2 cups saltine cracker crumbs or
    seasoned Italian bread crumbs
1 cup cheddar cheese, grated
1 teaspoon onion salt
1 tablespoon vegetarian Worcestershire sauce*
1/4 teaspoon garlic powder
1 tablespoon soy sauce
1/2 teaspoon liquid smoke seasoning or
    1 1/2 teaspoons Old Hickory Smoked Salt

Roll into walnut-sized balls. Bake 20 minutes at 400°F. If freezing, bake the meatballs only 15 minutes at 400°F. Cool and quick freeze the meatballs. They can then be placed in freezer bags. The sauce can be made several days before needed. To prepare for serving, put meatballs in casserole dish. Cover with sauce and bake at 350°F for 30 to 40 minutes.

Barbecue Sauce

PER SERVING	
Calories:	406
Total Fat:	24g
Cholesterol:	63mg
Sodium:	1298mg
Carbs:	37g
Protein:	15g

2 tablespoons butter or margarine
3/4 cup sliced onion
1 1/2 cups ketchup
4 1/2 teaspoons chili powder
3/4 cup brown sugar
9 tablespoons vegetarian
    Worcestershire sauce*
1 1/2 teaspoons salt
Dash of liquid smoke or
    3/4 teaspoon Old Hickory
    Smoked Salt

Sauté the onion in the butter. Add the ketchup, chili powder, brown sugar, Worcestershire sauce, salt, and liquid smoke. Simmer 5 minutes.

* *A note from Jackie:* If vegetarian Worcestershire sauce is unavailable, try substituting the following for 1 tablespoon of Worcestershire: 1 teaspoon soy sauce, 2 teaspoons balsamic vinegar or lemon juice, 1/2 teaspoon sugar, and a dash of cayenne pepper. Or, you may delete the Worcestershire sauce altogether and, for flavor, use seasoned Italian bread crumbs and processed cheese (refrigerate first for easy grating).

Ellen's Potato Casserole

serves 8

6 to 8 medium potatoes (cooked in the skins);
    cooled, peeled, and shredded
2 cups shredded cheddar cheese
2 cups light sour cream
1/4 cup melted butter or margarine
1/3 cup chopped green onions (use some of the firm green for color)
1 1/2 teaspoons salt

PER SERVING	
Calories:	339
Total Fat:	18g
Cholesterol:	59mg
Sodium:	676mg
Carbs:	32g
Protein:	12g

Mix all ingredients. Bake in a 9" x 13" pan or casserole dish, at 350°F for 35 to 40 minutes, or until golden and slightly crispy on edges. *This casserole can be made a day ahead and refrigerated. On the day of serving, bake as directed.*

A note from Ellen: I have yet to meet the person who doesn't like this dish!

Peas With Dill

serves 8

1/4 cup chopped onion
2 tablespoons butter or margarine
3 cups cooked fresh or frozen peas
2 tablespoons diced pimiento
3/4 teaspoon dill weed or fresh dill
1/8 teaspoon salt

PER SERVING	
Calories:	*76*
Total Fat:	*3g*
Cholesterol:	*0mg*
Sodium:	*86mg*
Carbs:	*9g*
Protein:	*3g*

Sauté onion in butter until tender. This may be done the day ahead. Stir in remaining ingredients. Cook until thoroughly heated.

Carrots w/Lemony Honey-Mustard Sauce

serves 6

2 tablespoons butter or margarine, softened
2 teaspoons prepared mustard
1 tablespoon honey
1/2 teaspoon fresh grated lemon peel
2 teaspoons lemon juice
1 pound cooked carrots
Chopped parsley

PER SERVING	
Calories:	*81*
Total Fat:	*4g*
Cholesterol:	*11mg*
Sodium:	*93mg*
Carbs:	*11g*
Protein:	*1g*

In a saucepan, blend butter and mustard. Stir in honey, lemon peel and juice. Heat. Pour over cooked carrots. Sprinkle with parsley.

Cucumber Cream Salad

makes 4 cups, or 8 side servings

1 3-ounce package lime gelatin
1 teaspoon salt
1 cup boiling water
2 tablespoons vinegar or lemon juice
1 teaspoon grated onion

1 cup light sour cream
1/2 cup mayonnaise
2 cups drained, minced cucumbers
   (remove seeds)

PER SERVING	
Calories:	95
Total Fat:	5g
Cholesterol:	5mg
Sodium:	408mg
Carbs:	13g
Protein:	1g

This salad may be made the day before serving it. Dissolve gelatin and salt in boiling water. Add vinegar or lemon juice, and onion. Chill until very thick. Blend in sour cream and mayonnaise, then fold in cucumbers. Chill until firm.

Garlic Bread With Oregano and Parmesan

3/4 cup olive oil
5 to 8 large garlic cloves, minced
2 teaspoons dried oregano
2 1-pound french bread baguettes, split lengthwise
3/4 cup freshly grated Parmesan cheese

PER SERVING	
Calories:	76
Total Fat:	3g
Cholesterol:	0mg
Sodium:	86mg
Carbs:	9g
Protein:	3g

Mix oil, garlic, and oregano in small bowl. Brush onto cut side of bread. Sprinkle with cheese.

This bread can be prepared the day ahead. On the day of serving, preheat the oven to 350°F. Place loaves, cheese side up, on a heavy baking sheet. Bake until cheese melts and bread is crusty, about 15 minutes.

Fudge Brownie Pie

serves 8

2 eggs or
    1/2 cup Morningstar Farms®
    Scramblers®
1 cup sugar
1/4 teaspoon salt
1/2 cup butter, melted

1 teaspoon vanilla
1/2 cup unsifted all-purpose flour
1/3 cup cocoa
1/2 cup chopped nuts (optional)
Ice cream
Hot Fudge Sauce (recipe follows)

PER SERVING	
Calories:	305
Total Fat:	13g
Cholesterol:	53mg
Sodium:	229mg
Carbs:	43g
Protein:	5g

Beat eggs in small mixer bowl, blend in sugar and melted butter or margarine. Combine flour, cocoa, and salt; add to butter or margarine mixture. Stir in vanilla and nuts. Pour into lightly greased 8-inch pie pan. Bake at 350°F for 25 to 30 minutes, or until almost set (pie will not test done). Cool, cut into wedges. Serve topped with ice cream and Hot Fudge Sauce.

Hot Fudge Sauce

3/4 cup sugar
1/2 cup cocoa
1 5-ounce can nonfat evaporated milk

1/3 cup light corn syrup
1/3 cup butter
1 teaspoon vanilla

PER SERVING	
Calories:	197
Total Fat:	8g
Cholesterol:	<1mg
Sodium:	134mg
Carbs:	32g
Protein:	2g

Combine sugar and cocoa in small saucepan, blend in evaporated milk and corn syrup. Cook over medium heat, stirring constantly, until mixture boils; boil and stir 1 minute. Remove from heat; stir in butter and vanilla. Serve warm.

Note: This recipe uses a small can of evaporated milk, not the regular size.

Fizzy Cranberry-Lemonade Punch

makes about 9 cups, or 12 servings

4 cups cranberry juice cocktail
1 6-ounce container frozen lemonade concentrate, thawed
1 liter seltzer or club soda, chilled
1 small orange, cut into 1/4-inch-thick slices, then each slice cut in half
Ice cubes (optional)

In large pitcher, stir together cranberry juice cocktail and undiluted lemonade concentrate, until blended. Stir in seltzer and ice cubes. Garnish with orange slices.

A note from Ellen: You can blend most of this drink a day ahead and keep it chilled, but don't add the cold seltzer and ice cubes until just before serving.

Yummy Stuffed Green Peppers

Cooked Carrots

Tasty Coleslaw With
   Sharon's Coleslaw Dressing

Creamy Pinto Beans

Bread Machine Whole Wheat
   Dinner Rolls

Water with lemon wedge

Blueberry Cream Dessert

SABBATH DINNER MENU #10

Contributed by Sharon Haas
Jamestown, North Dakota

Sharon says: I like to serve cooked carrots and coleslaw with stuffed peppers, and many times, I also serve the Creamy Pinto Beans.

Yummy Stuffed Green Peppers

serves 10

10 medium-sized green peppers,
   seeded, tops removed
6 to 7 cups boiling, salted water
1 1/2 tablespoons olive oil
1 20-ounce can Worthington® *Vegetarian Burger*®
1 large onion
2 cloves garlic

1/2 cup celery
1/2 cup carrots
2 packets beef-like seasoning and broth mix
4 cups cooked rice
2 15-ounce cans tomato sauce
Salt and seasoned salt to taste

Heat oven to 350°F. Cut thin slice from stem end of each pepper. Remove all seeds and membranes. Wash inside and out. Cook peppers in the boiling, salted water for 3 to 5 minutes. Drain.

Sauté vegetables and burger until vegetables are tender, add seasonings, rice, and one 15-ounce can tomato sauce. Lightly stuff each pepper with rice-burger mixture. Stand peppers upright in ungreased baking dish. Pour remaining tomato sauce over each pepper. Cover and bake 4 minutes, then uncover and bake 15 minutes longer.

This can be made the day before, covered, and placed in refrigerator. When ready to bake, just top with sauce and bake as indicated above.

PER SERVING

Calories:	*227*
Total Fat:	*5g*
Cholesterol:	*0mg*
Sodium:	*811mg*
Carbs:	*34g*
Protein:	*13g*

Cooked Carrots

serves 8

8 to 10 carrots, peeled and sliced
1 tablespoon butter
1 1/2 tablespoons brown sugar

Place in a medium saucepan, barely cover with salted water. Cook until tender. Drain and add butter and brown sugar. Serve.

Tasty Coleslaw w/Sharon's Coleslaw Dressing

serves 8

Finely shred 1 medium head cabbage and cover with the following dressing, using as much as you like.

PER SERVING	
Calories:	*233*
Total Fat:	*15g*
Cholesterol:	*0mg*
Sodium:	*530mg*
Carbs:	*25g*
Protein:	*2g*

Scant 1/2 cup vegetable oil
3/4 cup mayonnaise-like
  salad dressing and
  low fat mayonnaise mixture
2 tablespoons vinegar or lemon juice

1 teaspoon mustard
1/2 cup sugar
1 teaspoon salt
2 tablespoons minced onion

Place all ingredients in blender and blend briefly.

A note from Sharon: Don't use olive or canola oil because they separate. This dressing keeps for several weeks in the refrigerator.

Creamy Pinto Beans

serves 10

6 cups cooked pinto beans, drained (3 cups dry beans)
3/4 to 1 cup brown sugar (according to your taste)
1/3 cup ketchup
1/2 teaspoon dry mustard
2 1/2 tablespoons flour
2 cups cream

PER SERVING	
Calories:	232
Total Fat:	6g
Cholesterol:	18mg
Sodium:	297mg
Carbs:	37g
Protein:	9g

Mix all together and cook slowly until bubbly and slightly thickened.
Make it the day before, and just reheat.

Bread Machine Whole Wheat Dinner Rolls

makes 18 rolls

Combine the following in bread machine bucket:

1 1/2 cups warm water
2 1/2 cups whole wheat flour
1 cup white flour
3 tablespoons honey

1 teaspoon salt
2 tablespoons olive oil
2 tablespoons dough enhancer
1 1/2 teaspoons yeast

Return to bread machine and start process, choosing Dough on the menu (or stop before it goes into the baking cycle). Remove from the machine and form into dinner rolls. Place on greased pan to rise. When doubled in size, bake in preheated oven at 350°F, for 20 to 25 minutes.

Blueberry Cream Dessert

serves 12

1 1/2 cups graham cracker crumbs
1 1/3 cups sugar, divided
7 tablespoons butter or margarine, melted
1 1/2 cups cold water
2 envelopes unflavored gelatin
1 teaspoon vanilla
3/4 cup light sour cream
3 8-ounce containers blueberry yogurt
2 cups fresh blueberries
1 cup whipped cream or whipped topping

PER SERVING	
Calories:	*303*
Total Fat:	*11g*
Cholesterol:	*9mg*
Sodium:	*197mg*
Carbs:	*48g*
Protein:	*5g*

Combine the graham cracker crumbs, 1/3 cup sugar, and margarine. Pat into a 10" x 13" pan, reserving 1/4 cup of crumbs for the topping. Bake at 350°F for 10 to 12 minutes. Cool.

Combine remaining 1 cup sugar, water, and unflavored gelatin in a small saucepan. Heat until gelatin dissolves. Set aside to cool.

When the gelatin mixture is cool, stir in sour cream, vanilla, and blueberry yogurt. When partially set, add fresh blueberries and whipped cream or whipped topping. Pour onto cooled crust and top with crumbs. Refrigerate.

A note from Sharon: I make this dessert the day before serving, and it keeps well.

Sabbath Dinner Menu #11

Contributed by Ruth Murrill
Deltona, Florida

Jackie says: I first met Ruth when we arrived in Burma in 1953. I recognized her face as someone I had seen on the campus of Union College a few years earlier, and it warmed my heart. Ruth taught me the tricks of cooking from "scratch" in the mission field, and we have been close friends through the years. She loves to cook and loves to entertain, so you will enjoy her recipes, I know.

Ruth says: I make the Heavenly Casserole, Twice-baked Potatoes, and the Pineapple and Carrot Gelatin Salad on Friday. The casseroles may be baked on Friday and warmed on Sabbath, or they can be baked on Sabbath. I always make the tossed salad on Sabbath morning and omit the tomatoes until ready to serve. If covered with plastic wrap, it keeps well until lunchtime.

Heavenly Casserole

Twice-baked Potatoes

Harvard Beets

Cooked green beans

Tossed salad

Pineapple and Carrot Gelatin Salad

Juice

Rolls

Cherry Angel Dessert

Heavenly Casserole

serves 10

2 cups cooked rice
2 cups Worthington® *Diced Chik®*,
 including broth from can
1 cup chopped celery
1/2 cup chopped onion
1 10.75-ounce can low-fat
 condensed cream of mushroom
 soup, undiluted

1 4-ounce can mushrooms
1/3 cup 2% milk
1/2 cup light mayonnaise
1/2 teaspoon salt
1 cup grated cheese
1/2 cup slivered almonds

PER SERVING	
Calories:	218
Total Fat:	13g
Cholesterol:	14mg
Sodium:	612mg
Carbs:	16g
Protein:	9g

Mix all ingredients (except cheese and almonds) and pour into a greased 9" x 13" casserole dish. Garnish the top with grated cheese and slivered almonds. Bake at 350°F for 45 minutes.

Twice-baked Potatoes

serves 8

4 large baking potatoes,
 baked and halved lengthwise
2 tablespoons butter or margarine

1/2 cup hot 2% milk
1 teaspoon salt
1 cup grated cheese

PER SERVING	
Calories:	201
Total Fat:	8g
Cholesterol:	24mg
Sodium:	425mg
Carbs:	26g
Protein:	6g

Scoop out the potato pulp, mash, and mix with butter, milk, and salt. Beat until light and fluffy. Spoon potato mixture back into the shells and sprinkle with cheese. Reheat in oven until top is slightly brown. Before serving, sprinkle with chopped chives. *These can be prepared on Friday and baked the second time on Sabbath.*

Harvard Beets

serves 8

1/4 cup sugar
1 tablespoon cornstarch
1/4 cup lemon juice
Juice of 1 orange

1/4 cup liquid from beets
1 tablespoon butter or margarine
1 15-ounce can diced beets

PER SERVING	
Calories:	64
Total Fat:	2g
Cholesterol:	4mg
Sodium:	150mg
Carbs:	13g
Protein:	1g

Combine sugar, cornstarch, lemon juice, orange juice, and beet liquid in a saucepan. Cook until thickened. Add margarine and beets and heat thoroughly. Salt to taste. *Prepare on Friday and reheat on Sabbath.*

Pineapple and Carrot Gelatin Salad

serves 8

1 6-ounce package orange gelatin
2 cups boiling water
1 cup light sour cream
1 13 1/2-ounce can pineapple (do not drain)
2 cups grated carrots
1/2 cup nuts, chopped

PER SERVING	
Calories:	260
Total Fat:	12g
Cholesterol:	21mg
Sodium:	97mg
Carbs:	34g
Protein:	7g

Dissolve gelatin in boiling water. Stir in sour cream, pineapple and juice, carrots, and nuts. *Prepare on Friday.* Cover with plastic wrap and refrigerate.

Cherry Angel Dessert

serves 8

1 angel food cake
1 1-pound, 14-ounce can cherry pie filling (reserve 1/3 cup)
1 3.4-ounce package instant vanilla pudding
1 1/2 cups 2% milk*
1 cup light sour cream*

PER SERVING

Calories:	339
Total Fat:	4g
Cholesterol:	13mg
Sodium:	554mg
Carbs:	70g
Protein:	6g

Cut or tear cake into bite-sized pieces. Place 1/2 of the pieces in a serving bowl, or 9-inch pan. Spoon all but 1/3 cup cherry pie filling over half the cake pieces. Add the rest of the cake pieces on top of the filling. Combine the pudding, milk, and sour cream. Beat until smooth. Spoon over the cake and chill several hours, or overnight. Garnish with whipped topping and the rest of the cherries.

* As an alternative, you can use 2 cups of milk instead of the 1 1/2 cups milk and sour cream, and add some whipped topping to the pudding mixture.

SABBATH DINNER MENU # 12

Submitted by Naomi Wilmot
Grand Terrace, California

Naomi says: Some of these recipes I have had for years and have changed and adapted them to the area where we were living, or tried to use ingredients that are more healthful. I prepare the Pecan Roast, the Potato Casserole, and the Scalloped Corn a day or two ahead and refrigerate until Sabbath morning, then bake them in the same oven.

Jackie says: You'll love Naomi's Pear-Lime-Tofu Gelatin Salad. And you'll never know the tofu is in there, but it adds good protein.

Tip from Naomi: While the guests are waiting for dessert to be served, it is nice to set a dish of mixed nuts on the table for them to munch on.

Pecan Roast

Potato Casserole

Scalloped Corn

Pear-Lime-Tofu Gelatin Salad

Steamed broccoli with lemon wedges

Relish plate with olives, pickles, and crunchy vegetables

Lemon Glaze Cake

Pecan Roast

serves 12

5 cups Kellogg's® *Corn Flakes*®
2 cups finely chopped pecans
1 teaspoon garlic powder
1 teaspoon poultry seasoning
2 packets beef-like seasoning and broth mix
2 cups 2% milk
1/4 cup olive oil
1 large onion, chopped
4 ounces Worthington® Meatless Smoked Turkey (frozen), thawed and shredded
4 ounces Worthington® Meatless Chicken (frozen), thawed and shredded
2 eggs, beaten or 1/2 cup Morningstar Farms® *Scramblers*®
Salt to taste

PER SERVING	
Calories:	289
Total Fat:	22g
Cholesterol:	39mg
Sodium:	321mg
Carbs:	18g
Protein:	8g

Put Kellogg's® *Corn Flakes*® in bowl. Add pecans, seasonings, and milk. Let soak. Sauté onion to a light brown in the oil. Add this to other ingredients, along with shredded turkey and chicken. Add eggs and mix. Pour into 2-quart oiled flat baking dish and bake until brown at 350°F, about 45 to 55 minutes.

Set the oven for this to be finished baking about 15 minutes before you plan to serve dinner. Take out of the oven and allow to set at room temperature until serving.

Potato Casserole

serves 10

1 large onion, chopped
1/4 stick butter or margarine
8 to 10 large potatoes, boiled in
 the skins, peeled, and diced
1/2 pound Colby cheese, grated
1 2-ounce jar chopped pimiento

1/2 cup seasoned stuffing mix
3/4 cups 2% milk
1/4 cup light sour cream
1/2 teaspoon garlic powder
Seasoned salt to taste
Salt to taste

PER SERVING	
Calories:	258
Total Fat:	11g
Cholesterol:	31mg
Sodium:	210mg
Carbs:	32g
Protein:	9g

Sauté onion in butter or margarine. Mix with other ingredients and pour into greased casserole. Bake covered at 350°F for about 45 minutes. Uncover and bake another 15 minutes, or until top is lightly browned.

Scalloped Corn

serves 8

4 cups fresh or frozen corn
2 tablespoons butter or margarine
1/2 green pepper, chopped
1/2 onion, minced
3 tablespoons flour

1 teaspoon salt
2 eggs, beaten or
 1/2 cup Morningstar Farms®
 Scramblers®
1 cup 2% milk

PER SERVING	
Calories:	142
Total Fat:	5g
Cholesterol:	64mg
Sodium:	357mg
Carbs:	21g
Protein:	5g

If using fresh corn, boil whole ears until tender, then scrape kernels off of the cobs. Sauté green pepper and onion in butter or margarine for about 5 minutes, stirring constantly. Add flour and salt; stir until blended. Combine eggs, milk, and corn; add gradually to green pepper mixture. Pour into an oiled baking dish. Bake at 350°F until set, about 45 to 50 minutes.

Pear-Lime-Tofu Gelatin Salad

serves 10

3 cups pear juice
   (reserved juice + water)
1 6-ounce package lime gelatin
2 15-ounce cans pears,
   drained (reserve juice)

8 ounces firm tofu
2 tablespoons lemon juice
8- to 12-ounce container
   light whipped topping, thawed

PER SERVING	
Calories:	*182*
Total Fat:	*1g*
Cholesterol:	*1mg*
Sodium:	*143mg*
Carbs:	*26g*
Protein:	*19g*

Bring pear juice and water to a boil; add gelatin and stir until dissolved. Allow to partially set. Blend pears and tofu in blender; add lemon juice. Combine with gelatin; fold in whipped topping. Pour into a pretty crystal bowl to set. To serve, place a dollop of whipped topping in the center, topped with a maraschino cherry. *Can be refrigerated for several days.*

Lemon Glaze Cake

serves 15

1 package lemon cake mix
1/3 cup Canola oil
3/4 cup apricot nectar
3 eggs, beaten or 3/4 cup
   Morningstar Farms® Scramblers®

2 teaspoons lemon juice
1/2 teaspoon lemon zest
2 cups powdered sugar
Juice of 2 lemons

PER SERVING	
Calories:	*268*
Total Fat:	*9g*
Cholesterol:	*43mg*
Sodium:	*232mg*
Carbs:	*46g*
Protein:	*3g*

Combine cake mix, oil, and nectar. Add eggs, 2 teaspoons lemon juice, and zest. Beat until combined. Bake in a 9" x 13" dish at 350°F for 40 to 45 minutes. Combine sugar and remaining lemon juice to make a glaze. Remove cake from oven; poke holes in the top with a fork. Pour glaze over the cake. *This cake keeps well, refrigerated, for several days.* Top with seasonal fresh fruit.

SABBATH DINNER MENU #13

Contributed by Ruth Sipkens
Yuma, Arizona

Ruth says: Since our retirement from the former Far Eastern Division to the American Southwest, life has made a complete change. After several years in the bustling city life of Singapore, we have had no trouble adjusting to the sunny, casual, slower pace of the Southwest. Although we have lots of potlucks to welcome our winter "snowbirds," we enjoy this simple Sabbath meal when at home.

Ruth's Tex-Mex Quiche

Endless Coleslaw

Vegetable of your choice

Chocolate Chip Oat-Nut Cookies

Ruth's Tex-Mex Quiche

serves 8

1 tablespoon olive oil
1/2 of 20-ounce can Worthington®
   Vegetarian Burger®
2 tablespoons taco seasoning
8 (approx.) sourdough bread slices, lightly buttered
1 4-ounce can chopped green chilies
1 4-ounce can sliced black olives

1 2-ounce jar chopped pimientos
1 cup shredded Monterey Jack cheese
1 cup shredded cheddar cheese
1 tablespoon all purpose flour
3/4 cup Morningstar Farms® *Scramblers®*
1 1/2 cups half-and-half or 2% milk

Fry the burger in olive oil on medium heat until slightly brown. Add taco seasoning. *Use enough bread to fit the casserole dish you plan to use.* Place buttered side down in the greased dish. Spoon the burger over the bread. Scatter the green chilies, olives, and pimientos evenly over the bread and burger. Combine the cheeses with flour and toss together; spread over the casserole. In a separate bowl, beat the eggs, salt, and half-and-half (or milk). Pour over cheese. Bake at 325°F for 45 to 55 minutes or until a knife inserted in the center comes out clean. Cool for 10 minutes before cutting.

A note from Ruth: Because this dish is best "freshly baked," I do the final assembly on Sabbath, but do as much preparation as possible before Sabbath. I have the bread buttered, placed in the casserole dish, covered with plastic wrap, and in the refrigerator. I have the burger already fried, seasoned with the taco seasoning, and in a covered bowl in the refrigerator. The cheese is grated, measured, and tossed with flour and salt. On Sabbath morning, I spread the burger mixture over bread; scatter relishes and cheese over burger; beat eggs with half-and-half or milk; pour them over all, then bake.

PER SERVING	
Calories:	323
Total Fat:	18g
Cholesterol:	113mg
Sodium:	897mg
Carbs:	21g
Protein:	20g

Endless Coleslaw

serves 10

3 pounds (1 medium head)
    cabbage, shredded
1/2 green bell pepper,
    finely chopped
1/2 red bell pepper, finely chopped
1 medium sweet onion,
    finely chopped
1 carrot, grated
6 red radishes, grated

Dressing:
1 cup lemon juice
    (fresh, if possible)
1/2 cup olive oil
1/2 cup sugar
1 teaspoon celery seed
1 teaspoon salt

PER SERVING	
Calories:	153
Total Fat:	9g
Cholesterol:	0mg
Sodium:	218mg
Carbs:	18g
Protein:	2g

Combine vegetables in a large bowl, toss together, and set aside.

In a stainless steel saucepan over moderate heat, bring DRESSING ingredients to a boil. Stir while cooking to dissolve sugar. Boil 3 minutes. Pour this hot dressing over the cabbage mixture and toss well. Let stand at room temperature 30 to 60 minutes, tossing occasionally. For best flavor, cover and refrigerate one to two days before serving. *This will keep in the refrigerator from 7 to 10 days. This recipe makes a lot and would work great for a potluck!*

Chocolate Chip Oat-Nut Cookies

makes 3 dozen

1 cup (2 sticks) softened margarine
1 1/4 cups firmly packed brown sugar
1/2 cup white sugar
2 eggs or 1/2 cup Morningstar Farms® *Scramblers*®
2 tablespoons milk
2 teaspoons vanilla
2 cups flour
1 teaspoon baking soda
1 1/2 cups raw quick or regular oats
1 12-ounce package chocolate chips
1 cup coarsely chopped walnuts (optional)

PER SERVING	
Calories:	193
Total Fat:	11g
Cholesterol:	12mg
Sodium:	102mg
Carbs:	24g
Protein:	3g

Heat oven to 375°F. Beat margarine and sugars until creamy. Add eggs, milk, and vanilla; beat well. In a separate bowl, combine flour, baking soda, and oats; add to egg mixture. Stir in chocolate chips and chopped walnuts. Drop by rounded tablespoonful onto ungreased cookie sheet. Bake for 9 to 10 minutes for a softer, more chewy cookie; or 12 to 13 minutes for a crisp cookie. Cool 1 minute on cookie sheet; transfer to wire rack. Cool completely and store—*if there are any left after the family finds them!*

S A B B A T H   D I N N E R   M E N U   # 1 4

Contributed by Ruth Krenzler
LaCombe, Alberta, Canada

Ruth says: Ever since our daughters, Gaylene, Donna Lee, and Janice were small, this has been our favorite Christmas dinner "turkey." Now it is our daughters' families' favorite too. Our favorite fruitcake is a recipe from Esther Chalmers's cooking class of 1955. It looks good and tastes good! For a dessert without sugar (for my husband), this carob cake is a recipe we like very much.

Mock Turkey Loaf

Mashed potatoes and gravy

Vegetable Medley of Carrots,
   Broccoli, and Cauliflower

Tossed salad

Cranberry sauce

Tropical Fruit Cake

Five Minute Carob Cake

Mock Turkey Loaf

serves 8

PER SERVING

Calories:	243
Total Fat:	14g
Cholesterol:	78mg
Sodium:	719mg
Carbs:	14g
Protein:	16g

1 20-ounce can Worthington®
   Vegetarian Burger® *
1 large onion, finely diced
1/4 cup oil
1 cup saltine cracker crumbs
1 teaspoon poultry seasoning

3/4 cup 2% milk
3/4 teaspoon salt
1 8-ounce package light cream cheese
3 eggs or 3/4 cup Morningstar Farms®
   Scramblers®

Mix all ingredients well and bake in an oiled 9" x 13" pan for 1 hour at 350°F.

A note from Ruth: I often substitute bulgar wheat for a half of the can of the burger. Add 1 cup boiling water to 1/2 dry bulgar wheat and gently cook 15 minutes. Turn off heat and let stand, covered, for 15 minutes more, until tender.

Vegetable Medley of Carrots, Broccoli, & Cauliflower

Friday preparation: Slice carrots into coins. Trim the long broccoli stems, peel, and cut into coins. Separate broccoli and cauliflower heads into flowerets. Put veggies in plastic bags and refrigerate.

On Sabbath: Combine the vegetables and use 1/2 cup water in a saucepan or steamer to cook until tender-crisp, about 4 minutes. Season with salt. *Colorful, nutritious, and delicious!*

Tropical Fruit Cake

serves 16

3 cups whole Brazil nuts
  (or substitute some walnuts)
1 1-pound package pitted dates
1 cup drained maraschino cherries,
  red and green mixed
1 1/4 cups all-purpose flour

3/4 cup (or less) sugar
1/2 teaspoon salt
3 eggs, beaten or
  3/4 cup Morningstar Farms®
  Scramblers®
Milk

PER SERVING	
Calories:	*348*
Total Fat:	*19g*
Cholesterol:	*40mg*
Sodium:	*93mg*
Carbs:	*44g*
Protein:	*7g*

Put nuts, dates, and cherries into a large bowl. Add flour, sugar, and salt. Mix, using your hands if necessary. Beat eggs very lightly and add to fruit-nut mixture; combine well. Add milk as needed to make a firm dough. Grease two small loaf pans and line with waxed paper. Divide dough in half and pat into lined pans. Bake at 300°F for 1 to 1 1/2 hours. Allow to cool before slicing. (Dough can also be baked in one larger loaf pan for 1 1/2 to 2 hours.)

Five Minute Carob Cake

serves 9

1 cup cold water
2/3 cup raisins
2 tablespoons carob powder
1/3 cup Canola oil
1 tablespoon lemon juice

1 teaspoon vanilla
1 1/2 cups flour
1 teaspoon baking soda
1/2 teaspoon salt
Nuts (optional)

PER SERVING	
Calories:	*182*
Total Fat:	*8g*
Cholesterol:	*0mg*
Sodium:	*271mg*
Carbs:	*26g*
Protein:	*3g*

In blender, process together water, raisins, and carob powder. Add oil, lemon juice, and vanilla. Pour into a large bowl and add remaining ingredients. Mix together gently. Pour into a greased 9-inch square pan. Bake at 350°F for 35 minutes.

Mom's Carrot Roast

Creamed Baby Peas

Green Bean Casserole

Tossed salad

Rolls

Banana Pudding Cake

SABBATH DINNER MENU #15

Contributed by Dorothy Erwin
Dewey, Arizona

Dorothy says: This carrot roast is different than most, and has been a family favorite for 61 years. An Adventist preacher's wife gave it to my mother when I was born.

Jackie says: Dorothy was a terrific support in helping me plan interesting Shepherdess meetings for the pastors' wives when we were in Oregon. She has always been very involved in nutrition schools wherever she and her husband were in the ministry.

Mom's Carrot Roast

serves 8

1/2 cup walnuts
1 onion, quartered
2 tablespoons olive oil
1 teaspoon salt
1 teaspoon sage

3 eggs or 3/4 cup
    Morningstar Farms® *Scramblers*®
2 cups grated carrots
1 to 1 1/2 cups Italian seasoned
    or plain bread crumbs

Friday preparation: Process walnuts, onion, oil, salt, sage, and eggs in blender. Combine with carrots, then add breadcrumbs. Place in a greased loaf pan or ring mold. Cover with foil and refrigerate.

On Sabbath: Place Carrot Roast pan in the oven inside a larger pan with water in it. Set automatic timer to bake at 350°F for one hour. *You will want the baking to continue for about half an hour after you return home to accommodate the Green Bean Casserole (see p. 62).* Remove foil during last 15 minutes of baking. Unmold onto a platter and garnish with fresh parsley. If using a ring mold, pour creamed baby peas in center of ring.

PER SERVING	
Calories:	158
Total Fat:	7g
Cholesterol:	80mg
Sodium:	647mg
Carbs:	19g
Protein:	6g

Green Bean Casserole

serves 10

2 14.5-ounce cans French-cut green beans, drained
1 10.75-ounce can low fat condensed
    cream of mushroom soup, undiluted
1/2 soup can of 1% milk
1/4 teaspoon garlic powder
1 32-ounce package frozen seasoned *Tater Tots*™
    (enough to cover green beans)

PER SERVING	
Calories:	*317*
Total Fat:	*19g*
Cholesterol:	*3mg*
Sodium:	*759mg*
Carbs:	*33g*
Protein:	*4g*

Friday preparation: Put green beans into casserole dish. Combine the mushroom soup, milk, and garlic powder; pour over green beans. Cover and refrigerate.

On Sabbath, as soon as you get home: Cover the green bean casserole with frozen *Tater Tots*™ and place in oven with the Carrot Roast. Bake for 30 minutes or until tater tots are browned. *While the baking finishes, prepare creamed baby peas and a tossed salad.*

Banana Pudding Cake

serves 15

1/2 to 3/4 cup mashed banana
1 package yellow cake mix
1 13-ounce box vanilla instant pudding mix
4 eggs, beaten or 1 cup Morningstar Farms® *Scramblers*®
1 cup water
1/4 cup Canola oil
1/2 cup finely chopped walnuts (optional)
1 16-ounce container prepared cream cheese frosting
1/2 cup flaked coconut

PER SERVING	
Calories:	381
Total Fat:	15g
Cholesterol:	57mg
Sodium:	394mg
Carbs:	60g
Protein:	4g

Blend banana, cake and pudding mixes, eggs, water, oil, and nuts (if desired) in a large mixing bowl. Beat 4 minutes on medium speed. Pour into greased 9" x 13" pan. Bake at 350°F for 50 minutes. *Do not under-bake.* Cool the cake in the pan on a rack. Top with cream cheese frosting, sprinkle with coconut.

Chicken a la King

Green peas

Baked yams, sweet potatoes,
  or squash

Relish tray or tossed salad

Chocolate Éclair Cake

SABBATH DINNER MENU #16

Contributed by Jeanne Jarnes
Caldwell, Idaho

Jeanne says: The summer Dave and I were married in Seattle, Washington, the Volunteer Park Church threw a joint shower for four August brides, wheeling in a wheelbarrow of gaily wrapped small appliances for each of us. We were thrilled when the evening's activities included cooking demonstrations. Berta Johnson demonstrated this Chicken a la King recipe for me to try in my new electric skillet. Since the only thing I really knew how to cook at that time was Mom's egg gravy, I readily incorporated this easy recipe into my small repertoire! It has been a family favorite ever since.

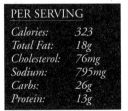

Chicken a la King

serves 6

1 12.5-ounce can Worthington® *FriChik*®, drained (reserve liquid) 1 tablespoon olive oil
1 4-ounce can mushroom pieces, drained (reserve liquid)
1 cup liquid (reserved liquid + water)
2 eggs or 1/2 cup Morningstar Farms® *Scramblers*®
1 onion, chopped

2 tablespoons flour
1 teaspoon curry powder
1 10.75-ounce can low-fat condensed cream of mushroom soup, undiluted
1 large can or bag of Chow Mein noodles or cooked brown rice

Drain *FriChik*® and mushrooms, reserving liquid, and combine liquid with water to make 1 cup. Break *FriChik*® into bite-size pieces.

Heat oil in nonstick skillet; add eggs and scramble, breaking up eggs into bite-size pieces as they cook. Push eggs to one side of pan and sauté the onion and mushrooms in the same pan. Stir eggs to brown lightly while onion and mushrooms sauté.

Sprinkle flour over eggs, onions, and mushrooms; add liquid. Stir to blend. Let simmer until flour is cooked and mixture is thickened to medium consistency. *Add more water if necessary.* Add curry powder and *FriChik*® pieces. Whip condensed cream of mushroom soup, undiluted in can, to make smooth; add to mixture in skillet. Heat, but do not boil. The mixture should not be too thin. Serve over crispy Chow Mein noodles or brown rice. *(Note: The nutritional analysis has been calculated using 1/2 cup Chow Mein noodles per serving. You can save calories and fat by using the brown rice instead!)*

PER SERVING	
Calories:	323
Total Fat:	18g
Cholesterol:	76mg
Sodium:	795mg
Carbs:	26g
Protein:	13g

3–S.D.C.

Chocolate Éclair Cake

serves 15

A note from Jeanne: Here is an easy dessert that looks and tastes like you spent hours slaving away in the kitchen. It is our son, Todd's, favorite.

21 sheets graham crackers (approx.)
1 8-ounce package low-fat
    cream cheese
3 1/2 cups 2% milk
2 3.4-ounce packages instant
    French vanilla pudding
1 8-ounce container
    light whipped topping

Chocolate frosting:
4 tablespoons warm milk
4 tablespoons butter
    or margarine, melted
4 tablespoons cocoa
1 3/4 cups powdered sugar

PER SERVING
Calories: 303
Total Fat: 11g
Cholesterol: 13mg
Sodium: 412mg
Carbs: 46g
Protein: 5g

Spray the bottom of a 9" x 13" glass baking dish with cooking spray. Line with graham crackers. In a 2-quart mixing bowl, mix cream cheese with a little milk. Gradually add rest of milk. Mix in pudding. Beat two minutes. Fold in whipped topping. Alternate layers of pudding with crackers. Ending with crackers on top. *You will have 3 layers of crackers, 2 layers of pudding.*

Prepare CHOCOLATE FROSTING by warming the milk and butter or margarine in microwave and stirring in the cocoa and powdered sugar. Cover top layer of cake with chocolate frosting. Refrigerate overnight. (I usually let the frosting set up in the refrigerator before covering loosely; otherwise the frosting will stick to foil or plastic wrap.)

Sabbath Dinner Menu #17

Contributed by Todd Jarnes
Berrien Springs, Michigan

Todd says: When I was a freshman at Andrews University, my roommate, Kaleb Cockrum, invited me to the Snorrasons' house for Sabbath lunch. This wonderful family from Iceland opened their home to students on a weekly basis and "adopted" several of us over the next few years. I distinctly remember invitations phoned in on Thursdays and anticipating Sabbath when we would arrive at the Snorrasons' and be greeted by open arms, smiling faces, a warm fireplace, nipping dogs, and heaping mounds of food. It wasn't only the food that we enjoyed, but also the games, walks, talks, and just good company. Although two thousand miles from Mom and Dad, I had another home, with ten brothers and sisters, surrogate parents, and surrogate dogs. "Who wants to say the blessing? OK, dig in!"

Jeanne says: Thanks to the Snorrasons for taking care of my boy all those years at Andrews! Todd often talked about the wonderful Majidra they served on Sabbaths. I can see why this meal would be perfect for groups large or small.

Majidra

White grape juice

Ice cream and cookies

Majidra

serves 8

2 1/2 cups dry lentils
10 cups water
6 cloves garlic
3 to 4 tablespoons beef-like
   broth and seasoning mix
2 1/2 to 3 cups rice,
   cooked per package instructions
2 to 3 cups chopped tomatoes

2 to 3 cups chopped cucumber
1 1/2 cups chopped onion
6 to 8 cups shredded lettuce
4 cups shredded cheese
1 cup fresh lemon juice
1 cup olive oil
1/2 teaspoon salt

Place lentils, water, garlic, and broth seasoning mix in large saucepan and bring to a boil. Lower heat and simmer until lentils are tender, approximately 1 hour (or longer if desired).

To serve, each person layers rice, lentils, cheese, and veggies onto his or her plate as desired. *The key to making this plateful of food absolutely mouth watering, according to Todd, is to use plenty of the "secret sauce" of lemon juice, oil, and salt. Best if served to starving hordes of college kids.*

PER SERVING
Calories:	323
Total Fat:	18g
Cholesterol:	76mg
Sodium:	795mg
Carbs:	26g
Protein:	13g

SABBATH DINNER MENU #18

Contributed by Nancy Beck Irland
Hillsboro, Oregon

Jackie says: Our daughter, Nancy, is an excellent cook and can get a meal ready in no time despite her very busy schedule as a nurse practitioner mid-wife.

Nancy says: As a working wife and mother, I don't always have time for exotic Sabbath meals. Here's a menu that is quick to throw together, yet looks and tastes like you spent hours on it. The meal is actually light, so the rich dessert complements it wonderfully. If you don't have time to bake the cake, then serve brownies or store-bought cookies and ice cream for dessert. I always prepare 2 quiches so the guests have a delightful variety of flavors. It fills them up too!

Spinach Mushroom Quiche

Almond Cauliflower Quiche

Fresh broccoli spears

Tossed salad with dressing

Garlic bread

Apple cider or sparkling cider

Luscious Cranberry Cake

Chamomile tea

Spinach Mushroom Quiche

serves 8

1 12-ounce frozen spinach soufflé*
2 eggs or 1/2 cup Morningstar Farms®
    Scramblers®
1 1/4 cups 2% milk (approx.)
1/4 cup mozzarella cheese, cut into chunks

4 Morningstar Farms® *Breakfast Links*®
    or Worthington® *Saucettes*®
1 4-ounce can mushroom pieces
Salt to taste
1 prepared pie crust

Thaw spinach soufflé. Meanwhile, crack 2 eggs into blender. Add milk up to the 1 1/2 cup measure line. Blend together, adding mozzarella cheese. Pour this mixture into mixing bowl. Add spinach soufflé, *Breakfast Links*® or *Saucettes*®, and mushroom pieces. Stir to combine.

Press pie crust into pie plate. Pour filling into the crust and bake at 425°F for 30 to 45 minutes, or until a knife inserted in center comes out clean and top is lightly browned. Cool slightly, cut into wedges, and serve.

Note: If you can't find frozen spinach soufflé at the store, add an extra egg and call it "Sausage Mushroom Quiche."

PER SERVING

Calories:	236
Total Fat:	14g
Cholesterol:	103mg
Sodium:	484mg
Carbs:	17g
Protein:	10g

Almond Cauliflower Quiche

serves 8

1 prepared, unbaked pie crust
1 1/2 cups fresh cauliflower flowerets
1/3 cup slivered almonds
3 eggs or 3/4 cup Morningstar Farms® Scramblers®
1 1/4 cups 2% milk (approx.)
1/4 cup light mayonnaise
1/4 cup grated Swiss cheese
1/4 cup grated cheddar cheese

PER SERVING

Calories:	244
Total Fat:	17g
Cholesterol:	93mg
Sodium:	245mg
Carbs:	15g
Protein:	8g

Press pie crust into pie plate. Steam cauliflower flowerets until barely tender. Drain and arrange evenly on crust. Sprinkle with slivered almonds. Crack 3 eggs into blender. Add milk to the 1 1/2 cup measure line. Blend together; add mayonnaise and cheeses. Pour over cauliflower and almonds. Bake at 425°F for 30 to 45 minutes, or until knife inserted in center comes out clean and top is slightly browned. Cool slightly, cut into wedges and serve.

Luscious Cranberry Cake

serves 15

1 cup granulated sugar
2 cups unbleached flour
1 teaspoon baking powder
1 tablespoon melted butter
1 cup 2% milk
3 cups whole cranberries

Sauce:
1/2 cup evaporated skim milk
1/2 cup sugar
1/2 cup butter or margarine

PER SERVING

Calories:	276
Total Fat:	10g
Cholesterol:	27mg
Sodium:	153mg
Carbs:	45g
Protein:	4g

Mix cake ingredients together and pour into greased 9" x 13" pan. Bake at 350°F for 30 to 45 minutes. Just before serving, combine SAUCE ingredients and bring to a boil. Pour hot sauce over individual servings. *Serve with chamomile tea and sugar and enjoy after-dinner conversation with your guests.*

SABBATH DINNER MENU #19

Contributed by Peter and Gayle Beck
College Place, Washington

Jeanne says: My brother, Peter, loves to cook and comes up with some wonderful concoctions! He helps his wife, Gayle, by planning and preparing dinner two nights a week. (Perhaps this love for cooking began when, as little missionary kids in Burma, my sister, Nancy, and I would include our baby brother in our forays into the kitchen. We loved to try recipes out of our set of Childcraft books—wonderful things such as eggnog with raw eggs that we proudly presented to Mom and Dad, who bravely took a sip and said a silent prayer for protection!) This menu is quick and easy to prepare—great for weekends when you haven't had time to do much on Friday!

Quick Greek-style Skillet Choplets®

Steamed broccoli

Tomato, cucumber, and sweet onion
    salad with Italian dressing

Pita bread and hummus

Sugar free fruit gelatin
    with whipped topping

Quick Greek-style Skillet Choplets®

serves 4

1 tablespoon olive oil
1 20-ounce can Worthington® *Choplets*®, sliced thinly
1 onion, halved and cut into thin wedges
2 garlic cloves, crushed through a press
1 6-ounce can tomato paste
2/3 cup water
2 tablespoons fresh lemon juice
1/8 teaspoon ground cumin
1/4 teaspoon ground cinnamon
3/4 cup crumbled feta cheese
1/2 cup coarsely chopped walnuts, toasted
3 tablespoons finely chopped fresh parsley

PER SERVING	
Calories:	264
Total Fat:	14g
Cholesterol:	17mg
Sodium:	799mg
Carbs:	12g
Protein:	23g

Heat oil on high heat until hot. Add *Choplets*® and brown. Remove and set aside. Put onion and garlic in the pan; cook over medium high heat, stirring, until onion is tender (3 to 5 minutes). Stir in tomato paste, water, lemon juice, cumin, and cinnamon. Stir while bringing to a boil. Reduce heat to low, cover, and simmer ten minutes, stirring once or twice. Return *Choplets*® to skillet and heat 1 to 2 minutes. Toss with cheese and walnuts and garnish with parsley. Serve over pasta or rice.

Hummus

(See Hummus recipe in *Adventist International Cookbook,* p. 149)

SABBATH DINNER MENU #20

Contributed by Carol Dodge
Meridian, Idaho

Jeanne says: Whenever Carol calls to invite us over for Sabbath dinner, we know we are in for a real treat! Her meals are not only delicious; they are served with simple elegance. In the spotless kitchen, everything is efficiently organized, and obviously prepared well ahead of time.

Mock Crab Cakes

Mashed potatoes

Egg Gravy

Steamed broccoli

Spinach Mandarin Salad
  With Garlic Dressing

Oatmeal Rolls

White grape and peach juice

Fruit Freeze

Mock Crab Cakes

serves 8

1 20-ounce can Worthington® Low Fat Vegetable *Skallops*®, ground
1 medium onion, chopped
2 tablespoons light mayonnaise
3 tablespoons mustard
4 eggs or 1 cup Morningstar Farms® *Scramblers*®
1 cup Italian seasoned bread crumbs
1 teaspoon Old Bay seasoning
2 tablespoons parsley

PER SERVING	
Calories:	186
Total Fat:	6g
Cholesterol:	108mg
Sodium:	683mg
Carbs:	15g
Protein:	18g

Combine all ingredients, fry into patties, and serve with tartar sauce.

Egg Gravy

serves 8

2 tablespoons Canola oil
1 egg or 1/4 cup Morningstar Farms® *Scramblers*®
1 1/2 tablespoons flour
1 packet beef-like broth and seasoning mix
1 cup 2% milk

PER SERVING	
Calories:	60
Total Fat:	5g
Cholesterol:	29mg
Sodium:	156mg
Carbs:	3g
Protein:	2g

Scramble egg well in hot oil. When cooked, use fork or potato masher to break into small pieces. Cover and let brown. Add flour and broth seasoning; mix well. Add milk slowly, stirring constantly until thickened.

Spinach Mandarin Salad

serves 8

8 cups fresh spinach, washed carefully, stemmed,
    and torn into bite-size pieces
1 11-ounce can mandarin orange segments, drained
1 red onion, sliced and separated into rings
1/4 cup slivered almonds, lightly toasted
Garlic Dressing (recipe follows) or Italian dressing

PER SERVING ·	
Calories:	171
Total Fat:	16g
Cholesterol:	0mg
Sodium:	186mg
Carbs:	7g
Protein:	2g

Just before serving, combine spinach, mandarin oranges, onions, and almonds; toss lightly with dressing.

Garlic Dressing

2 cloves garlic, crushed
1/2 cup olive oil
1/2 tablespoon salt

1/4 cup lemon juice
1/4 cup lime juice

Whisk together dressing ingredients in a measuring cup.

Oatmeal Rolls

makes 2 dozen

2 cups water
1 cup rolled oats
1 package yeast
1/3 cup lukewarm water

2/3 cup brown sugar
2 teaspoons salt
3 tablespoons oil
5 to 5 1/2 cups flour

Bring water to boil in medium saucepan; add oats. Remove from heat and let cool. Dissolve yeast in lukewarm water. Add sugar, salt, and oil to oats. Add dissolved yeast. Mix in flour. Knead lightly and let rise. Punch down and let rise again. Shape into rolls. If desired, you can dip tops lightly into water and then into poppy or sesame seeds. Let rise. Bake on greased cookie sheets 20 minutes at 375°F. For variation, cut the dough into large egg-size pieces. Roll into breadstick shape and tie in a knot to make a bow tie roll. *Baked rolls can be stored in freezer and warmed before serving.*

Fruit Freeze

serves 9

1 12-ounce box strawberries
3 medium bananas
1/4 cup lemon juice
1 1/2 cups orange juice

1/2 cup sugar
1 8-ounce container
   light whipped topping

PER SERVING	
Calories:	*134*
Total Fat:	*<1g*
Cholesterol:	*0mg*
Sodium:	*2mg*
Carbs:	*35g*
Protein:	*1g*

Mash strawberries and bananas. Add lemon juice, orange juice, and sugar. Mix. Place mixture in freezer until iced around the edges. Stir well, then freeze until firm. Remove from freezer about 15 minutes before serving. Cut into squares and serve with a dollop of whipped topping.

SABBATH DINNER MENU #21

Contributed by Susan Harvey
Boise, Idaho

Susan says: I found this recipe for stuffed cabbage in a bill from the Nashville Gas Company many years ago when I was new to cooking. Successfully adapting it to vegetarian burger took a few tries, but the final result went to many potluck Sabbath dinners at Nashville First Church.

Jeanne says: As Vice President for Marketing at Pacific Press®, Susan is always busy. However, she took time to submit several menus to this cookbook, all of which looked wonderful. We thought the stuffed cabbage was particularly yummy. And my guests were fighting over the last piece of Berry Lemon Tart when I tried it out!

Pennsylvania Stuffed Cabbage

Potato Supreme

Quick Glazed Carrots

Relish plate

Hot rolls

Berry Lemon Tart

Tropical Punch

Pennsylvania Stuffed Cabbage

serves 10

1 20-ounce can Worthington®
    Vegetarian Burger®
1 egg, well beaten or
    1/4 cup Morningstar Farms® *Scramblers®*
1/3 cup uncooked brown rice
2 packets brown beef-like broth or seasoning mix
2 tablespoons margarine or butter
2 medium onions, chopped fine
1 10.75-ounce can low-fat condensed
    tomato soup

1 10.75-ounce soup can of water
Juice of 1 lemon
1 teaspoon sugar
1 teaspoon salt
1 tablespoon parsley, minced
1/2 cup celery, chopped
10 medium-size cabbage leaves

In a large mixing bowl, combine the burger with the beaten egg, the uncooked rice, and brown broth seasoning. In a large frying pan, sauté onion in margarine or butter until translucent. Combine half of the onions with the burger mixture. Set aside.

To prepare the sauce, add the tomato soup and an equal amount of water to the remaining sautéed onion in the frying pan. Add the lemon juice, sugar, salt, parsley, and celery, and simmer for ten minutes.

Wash the cabbage leaves and boil gently in large saucepan until pliable, about five minutes. Divide the burger mixture into ten equal parts, and place one part of the burger mixture on each cabbage leaf. Loosely fold cabbage leaf around burger mixture envelope-fashion and secure with a toothpick.

PER SERVING
Calories:	161
Total Fat:	6g
Cholesterol:	28mg
Sodium:	546mg
Carbs:	17g
Protein:	11g

Place cabbage rolls seam side down in an electric skillet or ovenproof baking dish. Pour sauce over cabbage rolls. Cover pan tightly and cook slowly (200°F in an electric skillet, or 325°F in the oven), for one hour and 15 minutes. *Don't undercook—it takes this long to cook the rice.*

To serve on Sabbath, return to 325°F oven or reheat in 200°F skillet 15 to 20 minutes. Serve, spooning remaining sauce over cabbage rolls.

Potato Supreme

serves 10

6 unpeeled red or white potatoes
2 teaspoons olive oil
1/2 cup chopped onion
1/2 cup chopped green
    or red pepper
1/2 cup chopped fresh mushrooms
1 10.75-ounce can low-fat condensed
    cream of mushroom soup, undiluted
1/2 cup 2% milk or water
1/4 cup chopped fresh basil
    or 1 teaspoon dried basil
Salt to taste
3/4 cup grated cheddar cheese

PER SERVING	
Calories:	143
Total Fat:	5g
Cholesterol:	12mg
Sodium:	184mg
Carbs:	21g
Protein:	5g

Boil the potatoes until almost done. Cool, peel, and dice into a large bowl. Sauté onion, pepper, and mushrooms in olive oil. Add the vegetable mixture to the potatoes. Add the condensed cream of mushroom soup, milk or water, and basil. Mix together. Add salt to taste. Pour into a baking dish that has been sprayed with cooking spray. Sprinkle cheese on top. Bake at 350°F for about 30 minutes.

Quick Glazed Carrots

serves 6

1 pound package fresh peeled baby carrots
1 tablespoon granulated sugar
1 tablespoon margarine or butter

Friday preparation: Steam or microwave carrots until crisp-tender. Drain thoroughly (if necessary) and refrigerate.

On Sabbath: Remove carrots from refrigerator. Sprinkle sugar into a plastic bag. Shake carrots in sugar. Heat butter in a skillet. Add carrots and simmer just until glazed, turning often.

PER SERVING	
Calories:	54
Total Fat:	2g
Cholesterol:	6mg
Sodium:	47mg
Carbs:	8g
Protein:	<1g

Berry Lemon Tart

serves 8

Crust:
1 prepared pie crust
   (to fit 10-inch tart pan)
1 tablespoon sugar

Lemon filling:
3 egg yolks
1/4 cup sugar
1/4 cup fresh lemon juice
1 tablespoon grated lemon zest

4 ounces low-fat cream cheese, softened
4 ounces regular cream cheese, softened

Topping:
2 cups sliced fresh strawberries
1/4 cup fresh or frozen blueberries
3 tablespoons red currant jelly
1 tablespoon orange juice

PER SERVING	
Calories:	288
Total Fat:	17g
Cholesterol:	103mg
Sodium:	207mg
Carbs:	30g
Protein:	5g

CRUST: Heat oven to 450°F. Roll out crust, place in a 10-inch tart pan with a removable bottom. Press crust into bottom and up sides of pan. Sprinkle with 1 tablespoon sugar. Generously prick crust with a fork. If desired, place a piece of parchment paper on crust and weight down with pie weights or dried beans. Bake at 450°F for 9 to 11 minutes, until golden brown. Remove weights and set crust aside.

FILLING: In a small saucepan, combine egg yolks, sugar, lemon juice, and lemon zest. Whisk to mix well. Cook over medium-low heat, stirring constantly, for 7 minutes, until thickened. Remove from the heat and transfer to a medium bowl. Refrigerate until cool. Using an electric mixer, beat the softened cream cheeses together with the cooled lemon mixture until smooth and creamy. Refrigerate until ready to serve.

FRUIT TOPPING: Wash and slice strawberries. Wash and dry fresh blueberries. *If using frozen blueberries, remove them from freezer on Sabbath morning and place in refrigerator so that they will thaw slightly.*

Just before serving: Remove sides from tart pan, transfer tart to serving plate. Evenly spread lemon filling in a thin layer over crust. Arrange sliced fruit on top. In a small saucepan, heat currant jelly and orange juice. Drizzle over fruit. Garnish with mint leaves, if desired. Cut into wedges to serve.

Tropical Punch

Combine equal parts limeade, white grape juice, and ginger ale.

Sloppy Vegetable Sandwiches

Vegetable sticks

Tortilla chips

Rhubarb Crumble

SABBATH DINNER MENU #22

Contributed by Rena Glubay
Boise, Idaho

Rena says: This is an easy crockpot lunch and best if made at least a day in advance. It makes great leftovers too!

Be sure to have lots of napkins handy! And if it seems too sloppy, you can always eat it open-faced with a fork.

Sloppy Vegetable Sandwiches

serves 6

2/3 cup dry lentils, soaked overnight, rinsed, and drained
3 medium carrots, finely chopped
2 stalks celery, finely chopped
1 medium onion, finely chopped
4 cloves garlic, finely chopped
2/3 cup brown rice
2 tablespoons brown sugar
2 tablespoons Dijon mustard
3 1/2 cups vegetable broth
1 8-ounce can tomato sauce
2 tablespoons vinegar
Hamburger buns, French rolls, or pita bread

In a 4-quart crock-pot, combine all ingredients except the tomato sauce, vinegar, and bread. Cover and cook on low heat for 10 to 12 hours until lentils are done. Stir in tomato sauce and vinegar, cover, and cook for 30 more minutes. Spoon mixture onto bread and top with lettuce, tomato, and chopped onions (optional). Serve with sliced vegetables of your choice and tortilla chips. *This is actually better the second or third day, which makes it a great do-ahead recipe. If you have no crock-pot, you may cook this slowly on top of the stove, but may need to add two cups of water.*

PER SERVING	
Calories:	213
Total Fat:	2g
Cholesterol:	<1mg
Sodium:	868mg
Carbs:	42g
Protein:	10g

Rhubarb Crumble

serves 9

Pastry:
1/2 cup chopped nuts
   (pecans, walnuts, or both)
2 cups rolled oats
1/2 cup brown sugar
1/2 cup melted butter or margarine
2 teaspoons cinnamon
1 teaspoon vanilla

4 to 6 cups cut rhubarb
   (cut into 1/2-inch pieces)

Syrup:
1 cup sugar
3 tablespoons corn starch
1 1/2 cups water
2 to 3 teaspoons vanilla

PER SERVING	
Calories:	351
Total Fat:	16g
Cholesterol:	29mg
Sodium:	119mg
Carbs:	49g
Protein:	4g

Thoroughly mix PASTRY ingredients. *Pastry will remain crumbly.* Place one-half of the pastry in a 10-inch square or 8" x 11" pan. Press lightly. Place rhubarb on top. *You can mix rhubarb with strawberries, blueberries, or pineapple if preferred. The combined fruit should total 4 to 6 cups.*

Cook SYRUP in a medium saucepan until thickened. Pour hot syrup over rhubarb. Top with remaining half of pastry. Press lightly. Bake 40 to 45 minutes at 350°F. Serve warm or cool with vanilla ice cream.

SABBATH DINNER MENU #23

Contributed by Judy Jarnes
Bristol, Tennessee

Jeanne says: My sister-in-law, Judy, is one of those rare working women who still finds time to bake her own bread! She is a wonderful cook and always makes sure her guests are well fed. The Stuffing Casserole is a Jarnes tradition—no holiday dinner is complete without it. The cornbread stuffing gives it a special flavor and texture.

The Swedish Limpa Rye Rolls are also a Jarnes favorite—Mom Jarnes always made those for special weekends. We have all incorporated the recipe into our files. They are dark with molasses and rye and well worth the effort to bake!

Stuffing Casserole

Mashed Potato Casserole

Tossed salad

Snow peas

Swedish Limpa Rye Bread Rolls

Angel Food Strawberry Delight

Stuffing Casserole

serves 20

1 16-ounce cornbread stuffing mix
1 16-ounce herbed and seasoned bread stuffing mix
1 16-ounce roll frozen Worthington® *Chic-kettes*®,
    thawed and pulled apart into bite-size pieces
1 4-ounce can mushroom pieces and stems, drained (reserve liquid)
    and chopped fine
1 1/2 cups chopped celery
1 cup onion, chopped fine
1 cup melted butter or margarine
1 teaspoon chicken-like broth or seasoning mix
1 1/2 cups mushroom liquid (reserved liquid + 2% milk to make 1 1/2 cups)

PER SERVING

Calories:	267
Total Fat:	15g
Cholesterol:	30mg
Sodium:	749mg
Carbs:	23g
Protein:	10g

In a large mixing bowl, combine the stuffing mixes and *Chic-kettes*® pieces. Drain mushrooms, reserving liquid. Sauté celery, onion, and mushrooms in the butter or margarine. Add to the stuffing and *Chic-kettes*®. Mix well. Add the chicken-like broth or seasoning mix to the liquid and pour over the stuffing mixture, combining well. This makes a large amount. Divide into two 9" x 13" casserole dishes. *You may freeze one for future use. Cover with foil, wrap in a plastic garbage bag, and label. When ready to use, remove from freezer, thaw, and bake.* Bake at 350°F for 45 minutes to 1 hour. Baste with more milk if it appears too dry.

Mashed Potato Casserole

serves 12

12 to 15 large potatoes, peeled and cut into large cubes
1/2 stick butter or margarine
1 1-ounce package reduced calorie Ranch dressing mix
1 cup light sour cream

PER SERVING	
Calories:	258
Total Fat:	10g
Cholesterol:	29mg
Sodium:	371mg
Carbs:	38g
Protein:	4g

Boil potatoes in salted water until soft, 10 to 15 minutes. Drain and put in a large bowl. Add remaining ingredients. Mash and mix ingredients well. Put in greased 9" x 13" casserole dish. Bake for 1 hour at 350°F.

Swedish Limpa Rye Bread Rolls

makes 3 loaves

1 package dry yeast
1 teaspoon sugar
1/4 cup warm water
2 cups buttermilk
1 cup water
1/2 cup sugar
1 tablespoon salt
1/4 cup molasses
3 tablespoons oil
3 cups rye flour
5+ cups white flour

PER SERVING	
Calories:	288
Total Fat:	17g
Cholesterol:	103mg
Sodium:	207mg
Carbs:	30g
Protein:	5g

In small bowl combine first three ingredients; let stand until foamy. Put buttermilk in a large mixing bowl. Bring 1 cup water, 1/2 cup sugar, salt, molasses, and oil to a boil in a saucepan. Add to buttermilk. Stir in rye flour and mix well. Add yeast mixture. Add 5 cups white flour, or more if necessary to make a smooth dough. Knead well. Let rise until double, about 1 1/2 hours. Punch down, let rise again for about 3/4 hour. Form into three loaves, or two loaves and two pans of dinner rolls. Let rise again. Bake at 350°F for about one hour. *This bread freezes well.*

Angel Food Strawberry Delight

serves 12

1 loaf angel food cake
2 cups 2% milk
2 cups light vanilla ice cream
1 3.4-ounce box instant vanilla pudding
1 3-ounce box strawberry gelatin
1 cup boiling water
1 21-ounce can strawberry pie filling
1 8-ounce container light whipped topping

PER SERVING

Calories:	274
Total Fat:	3g
Cholesterol:	7mg
Sodium:	447mg
Carbs:	58g
Protein:	6g

Crumble or break angel food cake into a 9" x 13" pan. Using a hand mixer, combine milk with vanilla ice cream. Mix in vanilla pudding. Pour over cake pieces. Dissolve strawberry gelatin in boiling water. Add strawberry pie filling. When cool and just about set, pour over cake mixture. Refrigerate until ready to serve. Top with whipped topping.

Sabbath Dinner Menu #24

Contributed by DeAnne Aust
Juneau, Wisconsin

Kristi says: DeAnne is most definitely blessed with the gift of hospitality. On Sabbaths after church at Andrews University, there would often be a gang of us over at her house for dinner. She and I used to joke that I was Mary and she was Martha, because she would usually be busy in the kitchen while I worked oh-so-hard at keeping the guests company out in the living room where I could enjoy the conversation!

DeAnne says: The menu was usually determined by what we had in the house, and how long it had been since we'd gotten paid! Kristi's brother, Todd, and his friend Paul would usually stop by again later in the afternoon, whether or not they'd been at dinner, to check on the status of dessert. Leftovers were never a problem!

The main casserole in this menu comes from a good friend of mine who was also my roommate my senior year. The recipe was changed just a bit to

Chicken Casserole

Mixed green salad

Mashed potatoes and gravy

Steamed carrots and broccoli

Pistachio Torte

accommodate the allergies of another friend of ours. The following is really a combination of the two recipes, and in my opinion, the best of both worlds! Whenever I eat this, I am immediately transported back to our little yellow house with the crooked walls and floors filled with close friends who loved God and a warm meal outside of the cafeteria!

Chicken Casserole

serves 10

1/2 stick butter or margarine
1 medium onion, chopped
3 cloves garlic, minced
2 to 3 tablespoons chicken-like broth or seasoning mix
1 1/2 cups 2% cottage cheese
1 12.5-ounce can Worthington® FriChik®, drained and torn into pieces
3 eggs or 3/4 cup Morningstar Farms® Scramblers®
7 cups Kellogg's® Corn Flakes® (reserve 1 cup)

Sauté the first 4 ingredients together. Combine all ingredients and put into a 9" x 13" glass baking dish. Crush reserved 1 cup corn flakes on top. Cover and bake at 375°F degrees for 1 hour, then uncover and bake an additional 15 minutes until done.

PER SERVING

Calories:	223
Total Fat:	10g
Cholesterol:	67mg
Sodium:	589mg
Carbs:	22g
Protein:	12g

Pistachio Torte

serves 15

First layer:
1 cup flour
1 stick butter or margarine
2 tablespoons sugar
1/4 cup chopped nuts

Second layer:
1 8-ounce package low-fat
    cream cheese
1/2 of 12-ounce carton
    light whipped topping
2/3 cup powdered sugar

Third layer:
2 3.4-ounce packages
    instant pistachio pudding
2 1/2 cups 2% milk

PER SERVING

Calories:	303
Total Fat:	16g
Cholesterol:	12mg
Sodium:	316mg
Carbs:	33g
Protein:	5g

FIRST LAYER: Use a pastry blender to combine. Press into bottom of 9" x 13" dish. Bake 15 minutes at 375°F. *Do not overbake.* Cool.

SECOND LAYER: Blend ingredients. Once first layer is cooled, spread over cookie crust.

THIRD LAYER: Blend and chill until thickened. Spoon over second layer and smooth with spatula.

FOURTH LAYER: Spread the remaining half of the carton of whipped topping over the third layer.

FIFTH LAYER: Sprinkle with 1/2 cup chopped nuts.

Chill and serve.

Guatemalan Enchiladas

Oatmeal Raisin Cookies

Lemonade

Contributed by Loida Morales
Caldwell, Idaho

Jeanne says: No Pacific Press® cookbook would be complete without including one of Loida's recipes! Her reputation as a wonderful cook has spread far and wide—she caters our board luncheons and many other functions for distinguished guests such as literature evangelists and Adventist Book Center managers. In this menu, she shares a traditional meal from her husband's home country of Guatemala.

Guatemalan Enchiladas

serves 10

Pickling Mixture (recipe follows)
Salsa (p. 96)
1 cup chopped onion
1 cup chopped bell pepper
1/2 cup chopped celery
2 garlic cloves, chopped fine
1/4 teaspoon cumin

3 tablespoons chicken-like broth or seasoning mix
1 cup tomato sauce
1 cup water
1 20-ounce can Loma Linda® *Vege-Burger*®
20 crispy tortillas
6 hard-boiled eggs, sliced
Parmesan cheese

Pickling Mixture and Salsa are best when made several hours before serving or refrigerated overnight.

In large skillet sauté onion, bell pepper, celery, and garlic. Add seasonings, tomato sauce, water, and burger. Mix well and set aside.

Each person should individually layer enchiladas as follows:
Tortilla > burger > Pickling Mixture > Salsa > egg slices > sprinkle of Parmesan cheese

---

PER SERVING

Calories:	333
Total Fat:	10g
Cholesterol:	127mg
Sodium:	863mg
Carbs:	39g
Protein:	21g

Pickling Mixture

3 cups cabbage, chopped fine
1 cup grated carrots
1 14.5-ounce can French-cut green beans, drained
1 15-ounce can green peas, drained

1 15-ounce can julienne beets, drained
1/2 cup white vinegar
Salt to taste

Microwave cabbage and carrots for 4 minutes. Add remaining ingredients.

Salsa

1 bunch cilantro
2 14.5-ounce cans diced tomatoes
1 tablespoon chopped green onion
   or dry minced onion

1 teaspoon crushed
   chili pepper flakes
Salt to taste

Wash cilantro carefully, chop, and put in a bowl. Purée tomatoes (or use crushed tomatoes if you prefer); add to cilantro. Add onion, chili pepper flakes, and salt; mix well. *Add more pepper flakes for a hotter salsa.*

Oatmeal Raisin Cookies

makes 3 dozen

1 cup raisins
1/2 cup vegetable shortening
1/4 cup water
1 egg or 1/4 cup
   Morningstar Farms® Scramblers®
1 teaspoon vanilla
1 cup brown sugar

3/4 cup flour
1/2 teaspoon salt
1/2 teaspoon baking soda
1 teaspoon cinnamon
1 1/2 cups quick oatmeal
1 cup chopped walnuts
1 cup chocolate chips

PER SERVING	
Calories:	119
Total Fat:	7g
Cholesterol:	13mg
Sodium:	82mg
Carbs:	15g
Protein:	2g

Wash and drain raisins. In a saucepan, heat shortening and water until shortening is melted, stirring constantly. Add raisins. Let mixture cool. Add egg and mix well. Add vanilla and sugar; mix well. Sift together flour, salt, baking soda, and cinnamon; add to raisin mixture. Add oatmeal, walnuts, and chocolate chips. Drop rounded teaspoons of dough on cookie sheet and bake for 10 to 15 minutes at 350°F. Let cool.

Sabbath Dinner Menu #26

Contributed by Dorothy Lawson
Nampa, Idaho

Oatmeal Patties

Twice-baked potatoes (in the winter)
or potato salad (in the summer)

Any green vegetable

Sunshine Salad

Homemade bread or rolls

Sugarless Apple Pie

Dorothy says: Here is a favorite of ours for Sabbath! I sometimes use a Tomato Gravy made of tomato soup diluted with one can of water and about 1 tablespoon of Vegex® in it. Another option is to make a broth of water and Vegex®. They are both good.

I make Twice-Baked Potatoes by baking the potatoes on Friday and scooping out the "innards," which I then make into mashed potatoes. (Use whatever seasonings you like best.) I stuff the mashed potatoes back into the baked potato shells, cover and refrigerate until Sabbath. Bake for 20 to 30 minutes at 350°F.

The Sugarless Apple Pie is delicious and easy to make—my husband and I like it better than the regular kind.

Oatmeal Patties

serves 8

PER SERVING

Calories:	*192*
Total Fat:	*12g*
Cholesterol:	*57mg*
Sodium:	*302mg*
Carbs:	*15g*
Protein:	*9g*

1 cup quick oats
1 cup finely ground walnuts or pecans
1 small onion, chopped
1 teaspoon poultry seasoning
2 eggs or 1/2 cup Morningstar Farms®
    Scramblers®
1/4 cup 2% milk
    (add slowly—you may not need that much)

1 to 2 tablespoons light soy sauce
1 to 2 tablespoons Brewer's yeast
1 10.75-ounce can low-fat condensed
    cream of mushroom soup, undiluted
1 soup can water

Combine all ingredients except soup and water. The mixture should be quite moist—that can be controlled by how much milk you add. Fry patties in a small amount of vegetable oil. Combine mushroom soup and water and pour over the patties (or use one of the other sauce options mentioned above). Bake at 350°F until bubbly.

Sunshine Salad

serves 8

1 6-ounce package lemon gelatin
1 20-ounce can crushed pineapple, drained
1 cup grated carrots

PER SERVING

Calories:	*141*
Total Fat:	*0g*
Cholesterol:	*0mg*
Sodium:	*65mg*
Carbs:	*35g*
Protein:	*2g*

Mix gelatin as directed on package. Place in refrigerator and when it is soft-set, gently stir in the pineapple and carrots. Return to the refrigerator to finish setting.

Sugarless Apple Pie

serves 8

1 12-ounce can frozen apple juice, undiluted
7 cups (approx.) sliced Golden Delicious apples
2 tablespoons cornstarch
Cinnamon and margarine to taste
Unbaked pie crust for a two-crust pie

PER SERVING	
Calories:	413
Total Fat:	18g
Cholesterol:	0mg
Sodium:	281mg
Carbs:	61g
Protein:	3g

Cook the sliced apples in the apple juice until they can be pierced easily with a fork. Remove apples from the juice. Mix cornstarch into the juice and heat until thickened. Add margarine and cinnamon. Add apples to thickened juice and place mixture in unbaked pie crust that has been pressed into a 9- or 10-inch pie plate. Cover with the top crust and bake at 400°F until the crust is brown.

Vegetable Soup With Stuffed Pasta

Korean Spinach Salad

Bread

Cookies

SABBATH DINNER MENU #27

Contributed by Darlene McCart
Caldwell, Idaho

Darlene says: My friend Linda Sanders of Yuba City inspired the idea of a simple agape feast for Sabbath lunch. Combine this soup and salad meal with your choice of bread. A couple of my favorites are cornbread with honey butter (1 teaspoon of honey to each 1/4 cup of butter) or garlic bread (1/2 cup butter, 2 tablespoons Parmesan cheese, 1 teaspoon each dried parsley and garlic powder).

Vegetable Soup With Stuffed Pasta

serves 10

PER SERVING	
Calories:	192
Total Fat:	12g
Cholesterol:	57mg
Sodium:	302mg
Carbs:	15g
Protein:	9g

2 tablespoons olive oil
1 cup diced onion
1 cup diced carrots
1 cup diced celery
8 cups water
8 teaspoons chicken-like broth or seasoning mix
1 14.5-ounce can tomatoes, whole or diced
1 14.5-ounce can Italian stewed tomatoes
1 14.5-ounce can kidney beans, rinsed and drained
1 14.5-ounce can green beans, cut into bite-size pieces
1 7-ounce package stuffed ravioletti or cheese tortellini

Heat oil in frying pan. Sauté onions and celery in oil until soft. Add carrots; cook for 2 minutes. Add water and broth or seasoning mix and cook for 30 minutes over low heat. Add tomatoes, beans, and pasta; cook for 15 minutes, or until pasta is done. *This soup can be prepared ahead of time and stored in the refrigerator to reheat on Sabbath.*

Korean Spinach Salad

serves 10

1 pound fresh spinach
3 hard boiled eggs, sliced
8 slices Morningstar Farms®
    Stripples®
1 8-ounce can sliced
    water chestnuts, drained
1/2 pound mushrooms, sliced
2 cups fresh bean sprouts

Dressing:
1/2 cup olive oil
1/3 cup sugar
1/2 medium onion
1/4 cup vinegar or lemon juice
1/3 cup ketchup
1 tablespoon vegetarian
    Worcestershire sauce

PER SERVING	
Calories:	210
Total Fat:	15g
Cholesterol:	64mg
Sodium:	344mg
Carbs:	15g
Protein:	5g

Trim and discard rough spinach leaves and stems. Rinse well and pat dry. Break into bite-size pieces in salad bowl. Lay *Stripples®* in single layer on microwave-safe plate that has been sprayed with cooking spray. Microwave for 3 minutes or until crispy. Crumble into bite-size pieces and add to spinach. Add remaining salad ingredients. Blend DRESSING ingredients together. Toss salad with dressing just before serving.

SABBATH DINNER MENU #28

Contributed by Sara Sink
Berrien Springs, Michigan

Sara says: Here's a tasty nondairy Sabbath dinner idea. The Lemon Garlic Potatoes are especially low fat and simple to make. They are a wonderful accompaniment to any meal. The Lemon Parsley Dressing is nutritious and bursting with flavor. It makes tossed salads come alive, and can also be served over a variety of greens.

Stuffed Green Peppers

Lemon Garlic Potatoes

Broccoli

Tossed Salad With
   Lemon Parsley Dressing

French bread

Raisin Rice Pudding

Stuffed Green Peppers

serves 12

6 large green peppers, tops removed
3 tablespoons olive oil
3 garlic cloves, minced
1 large onion, diced
1 1/2 stalk celery, diced
1 cup Loma Linda®
    Vege-Burger® (optional)

2 1/2 cups diced canned tomatoes
1 8-ounce can tomato sauce
1/4 teaspoon thyme
1/4 teaspoon oregano
1 cup Italian seasoned
    bread crumbs
1 teaspoon salt

PER SERVING	
Calories:	*112*
Total Fat:	*5g*
Cholesterol:	*0mg*
Sodium:	*580mg*
Carbs:	*13g*
Protein:	*6g*

Parboil green peppers in for 5 minutes. Cool and scoop out seeds. Salt lightly, if desired.

In large frying pan sauté the garlic, onions, and celery in olive oil until tender. Add *Vege-Burger*®, if desired. Add remaining ingredients and stir until blended. Cut peppers in half and stuff with tomato mixture. Spoon any remaining mixture over peppers. Bake at 350°F for 30 minutes.

Lemon Garlic Potatoes

serves 8

2 cups boiling water
Juice of one large lemon
8 whole garlic cloves, peeled
2 tablespoons chicken-like broth
    or seasoning mix

1/4 teaspoon dried basil
1/4 teaspoon dried oregano
Salt to taste
6 large white or red potatoes,
    unpeeled and quartered

PER SERVING	
Calories:	*179*
Total Fat:	*<1g*
Cholesterol:	*0mg*
Sodium:	*13mg*
Carbs:	*41g*
Protein:	*4g*

Combine everything in a baking pan. Cover and bake at 350°F for 1 hour, basting occasionally with juice in pan. Uncover for the last 10 minutes of baking.

Broccoli

Steam broccoli flowerets and lightly toss with sautéed sesame seeds and sliced almonds.

Lemon Parsley Dressing

makes 2 1/2 cups (40 tablespoons)

1/3 cup olive oil
1/2 cup water
1/2 cup fresh lemon juice
1/2 cup bell pepper
1/2 cup fresh parsley

1 garlic clove
2 green onions
1/4 teaspoon Italian seasoning
Salt to taste

PER TABLESPOON	
Calories:	18
Total Fat:	2g
Cholesterol:	0mg
Sodium:	1mg
Carbs:	1g
Protein:	<1g

Combine all ingredients in blender and process until smooth. Toss with salad, the amount to use depends on how large a salad you make.

Don't forget to add the fun items to your salad—for example: toasted cashews, red onions, green olives, sunflower seeds, sesame sticks, and marinated tofu.

Raisin Rice Pudding

serves 8

2 cups water*
1/2 cup minute tapioca
1/3 cup sugar*
1/4 teaspoon salt
1 cup raisins
1 teaspoon vanilla

1 teaspoon cinnamon
1 tablespoon molasses
4 cups cooked rice
1/2 cup nuts (optional)
Whipped topping

PER SERVING

Calories:	250
Total Fat:	<1g
Cholesterol:	0mg
Sodium:	76mg
Carbs:	77g
Protein:	3g

SUGAR-FREE

Calories:	237
Total Fat:	<1g
Cholesterol:	0mg
Sodium:	75mg
Carbs:	56g
Protein:	3g

Soak tapioca in water for 5 minutes; add sugar and salt. Bring to a boil and simmer for 20 minutes. Stir in raisins, vanilla, cinnamon, and molasses. Add rice and mix again. Pour into an oiled serving dish and chill well. Serve individual portions garnished with a bit of molasses, a few walnuts, pecans, or peanuts if desired, and a dollop of whipped topping.

Sugar-free variation: Put a 12-ounce can apple juice concentrate into a two-cup measuring cup. Add water to equal 2 cups. Soak the tapioca in the apple juice for 5 minutes; add salt but eliminate sugar. *Proceed with recipe as written.*

SABBATH DINNER MENU #29

Contributed by Carole Hull
Hemet, California

Jeanne says: Carol definitely has the gift of hospitality! She and her husband, Bill were our pastoral team here in Caldwell, Idaho, for several years, and every Sabbath their home was filled with guests for dinner. This is one of her favorite menus.

Mock Salmon Loaf

Snow Pea Salad

Fresh steamed broccoli

Garlic-Herb Bread

Fresh strawberries
   over strawberry ice cream

Mock Salmon Loaf

serves 8

2 cups finely diced celery
2 12.5-ounce cans
   Worthington® FriChik®,
   drained and mashed or grated
1 cup light mayonnaise

2 cups dry bread crumbs
2/3 cup diced green pepper
1 diced onion
1 can Tartex vegetable paté
   (with paprika, if available)

PER SERVING	
Calories:	*296*
Total Fat:	*18g*
Cholesterol:	*10mg*
Sodium:	*750mg*
Carbs:	*24g*
Protein:	*12g*

Boil celery in unsalted water for 5 minutes, drain. Combine all ingredients, place in well-oiled bread pan. Bake 1 hour at 350°F. Invert on a platter and serve with tartar sauce.

Snow Pea Salad

serves 12

1 head cauliflower
1 pound fresh snow peas
   or two packages frozen
2 4-ounce cans sliced
   water chestnuts, drained
1 cup fresh, sliced mushrooms
1 2-ounce jar diced pimientos
4 tablespoons toasted sesame seeds

1/3 cup olive oil
2 tablespoons lemon juice
2 tablespoons vinegar
2 tablespoons sugar
2 cloves garlic, chopped
2 teaspoons salt
1/2 cup chopped green onions

PER SERVING	
Calories:	*120*
Total Fat:	*8g*
Cholesterol:	*0mg*
Sodium:	*418mg*
Carbs:	*1g*
Protein:	*4g*

Separate cauliflower into flowerets. Cook 3 minutes in 1/2 cup water and drain. Cook snow peas 1 minute and drain. Toss with other ingredients, chill, and serve.

Garlic-Herb Bread

makes 18 slices

1 stick (1/2 cup) margarine, softened
2 to 4 cloves garlic, minced
2 tablespoons chopped fresh chives
2 tablespoons chopped fresh parsley
1 loaf French bread

PER SLICE	
Calories:	*197*
Total Fat:	*8g*
Cholesterol:	*0mg*
Sodium:	*381mg*
Carbs:	*26g*
Protein:	*5g*

In a food processor, combine margarine, garlic, chives, and parsley. Process until smooth and well blended. Cut bread, almost through to the crust, into slices about 1-inch wide. Spread garlic butter in slits. Wrap bread in foil. If necessary, cut loaf in half and wrap each half separately. Bake 20 minutes at 400°F. For a crisp, golden crust, unwrap loaf for last 5 to 10 minutes of baking. This garlic bread is best served right out of the oven. *Note: I prefer to use whole wheat French bread.*

Matzo Balls

Mashed potatoes

Corn or green beans

Mandarin Orange Garden Salad
  With Poppy Seed Dressing

Rolls or bread

Chocolate Pudding and
  Vanilla Ice Cream

SABBATH DINNER MENU #30

Contributed by Julie Keener
Clovis, California

Julie says: With my hectic schedule, I need a company menu that doesn't require a lot of last-minute preparation, so I look for recipes I can make ahead. These have become favorite dishes, and they usually turn up at our table when we have company or family celebrations.

Matzo Balls

serves 10

2 cups Italian seasoned bread crumbs
1 1/2 cups chopped walnuts or pecans
1 1/2 cups grated jack cheese
3 teaspoons chopped onion

3 teaspoons parsley flakes
1/3 cup 2% milk
2 eggs or 1/2 cup Morningstar Farms®
    Scramblers®

Mix all the ingredients and form into balls. Place in a glass baking dish. They may be frozen at this point. When ready to bake, thaw and cover with Mushroom and Sour Cream Sauce and bake at 350°F for 30 to 40 minutes.

PER SERVING

Calories:	*339*
Total Fat:	*26g*
Cholesterol:	*84mg*
Sodium:	*509mg*
Carbs:	*17g*
Protein:	*12g*

Mushroom and Sour Cream Sauce

2 10.75-ounce cans low fat
    condensed cream of
    mushroom soup, undiluted

2 cups light sour cream
3/4 cup water

Mix together and pour over Matzo Balls.

Mandarin Orange Garden Salad

Simply make this salad as large or small as you wish with the following ingredients:

Romaine lettuce, torn into pieces
Mandarin oranges, drained

Red onion, chopped
Pine nuts

Poppy Seed Dressing

serves 16

This makes a large batch of dressing that you can divide in half if you prefer. But if you're making a big salad, this one is a crowd pleaser.

1/2 cup white onion, chopped
1/2 cup honey
1/3 cup lemon juice
1 teaspoon dry mustard (optional)
3/4 teaspoon salt

1 cup olive oil
   *(Lite version: 1/2 cup oil
   and 1/2 cup water)*
2 tablespoons poppy seeds

In blender, blend onions on medium speed. Add honey, lemon juice, mustard, and salt. While blending, slowly add oil mixture. Add poppy seeds and blend just until mixed. Store in refrigerator until ready to serve. Toss with salad just before serving.

PER SERVING	
Calories:	*160*
Total Fat:	*14g*
Cholesterol:	*0mg*
Sodium:	*110mg*
Carbs:	*10g*
Protein:	*<1g*

LITE VERSION	
Calories:	*100*
Total Fat:	*7g*
Cholesterol:	*0mg*
Sodium:	*110mg*
Carbs:	*10g*
Protein:	*<1g*

Chocolate Pudding and Vanilla Ice Cream

Use old-fashioned cook-and-serve chocolate pudding. Prepare before meal. Pour warm pudding over vanilla ice cream.

SABBATH DINNER MENU #31

Contributed by Rae Lee
Magalia, California

Rae says: This meal is our Christmas dinner or Christmas Sabbath dinner. I believe that Mom got this "chicken" loaf recipe from Naomi Yamashiro during the years we lived in Hawaii. Mom made it often at home and later, whenever she and Daddy came to visit in our homes, she would bring this loaf with her. The Roasted Potatoes and Onions recipe is part of my husband, Paul's, Australian heritage. The Australians usually have a roast dinner for the holidays. Carrots and/or sweet potatoes can also be included.

Jeanne says: Rae is a dietitian for the State of California. She and I started swapping recipes 20 years ago when we were neighbors in student housing at Andrews University!

Mom's "Chicken" Loaf

Red and White Roasted Potatoes

Broccoli Medley

Acorn Squash

Christmas Candle Salad

Grandma Ward's
    Pineapple Cranberry Mold

Cranberry Cake
    With Caramel Sauce

Mom's "Chicken" Loaf

serves 8

1 12.5-ounce can Worthington® *FriChik*®, drained and ground
1/2 cup grated mozzarella or jack cheese
1 3-ounce package light cream cheese
1/3 cup olive oil
2 cups soft bread crumbs or seasoned Italian bread crumbs
3/4 cup milk (evaporated skim milk is best)
4 eggs or 1 cup Morningstar Farms® *Scramblers*®
1 large onion, minced
1 tablespoon minced parsley

Mix all ingredients together. Pour into a greased loaf pan lined with waxed paper. Bake at 350°F for 1 hour. Let set in pan approximately 15 to 20 minutes. Turn out of loaf onto serving tray. Garnish with parsley. Serve with brown gravy.

Red and White Roasted Potatoes

serves 8

1 pound small red potatoes
1 pound small russet potatoes, peeled and cut in half
1 pound small onions, peeled
1/3 cup olive oil
Salt and other seasonings to taste

Wash potatoes and onions and place in zip-lock bag with oil. Shake until well-coated. Place into 9" x 13" casserole dish. Sprinkle on salt and other seasonings as desired. Bake uncovered at 350°F for one hour.

Broccoli Medley

serves 8

1 bunch broccoli (1 3/4 pounds)
2 tablespoons salad oil
1/4 pound mushrooms, quartered
1 onion, thinly sliced into rings
1 red pepper, julienned
1 8-ounce can whole
    water chestnuts, drained

3/4 teaspoon salt
1/4 cup rice vinegar
    or lemon juice
1 tablespoon dark sesame oil
2 tablespoons sliced almonds,
    toasted

PER SERVING	
Calories:	136
Total Fat:	7g
Cholesterol:	0mg
Sodium:	250mg
Carbs:	16g
Protein:	5g

Trim the broccoli and cut into flowerets. Peel the stems and cut crosswise into 1/2-inch pieces. Steam in 1/2 cup water for 3 minutes. Drain and place on serving dish. Keep warm. *You can also rinse the broccoli and stems, place in microwave-safe bowl and just before serving, microwave for 2 to 3 minutes or until crisp-tender.*

Heat oil, add mushrooms, onion, and pepper. Sauté until crisp-tender. Add water chestnuts, salt, vinegar, and sesame oil. Heat thoroughly. Pour over broccoli and sprinkle with almonds.

Acorn Squash

Slice acorn squash in half (or in thirds if large). Scrape out seeds. Place in pan with small amount of water on the bottom. Bake one hour at 350°F. The last few minutes of baking, fill with cranberry relish or marshmallows.

Christmas Candle Salad

A note from Rae: My grandmother always made this salad for Christmas dinner.

On individual salad plates place:

1 lettuce leaf
1 slice (ring) canned pineapple
1/2 banana *standing in the middle of the pineapple to make the candle*
1 maraschino cherry *on top of the "candle"*

Grandma Ward's Pineapple Cranberry Mold

serves 8

1 1/2 cups pineapple juice (reserved juice + water)
2 3-ounce packages lemon gelatin
1 20-ounce can crushed pineapple (reserve juice)
1/2 cup lemon juice
1/3 cup chopped walnuts
3 tablespoons shredded or chopped orange peel
3 cups whole cranberry sauce

PER SERVING	
Calories:	311
Total Fat:	3g
Cholesterol:	0mg
Sodium:	78mg
Carbs:	72g
Protein:	3g

Heat pineapple juice and water to boiling and pour over gelatin. Stir until completely dissolved. Stir in remaining ingredients. Pour into a mold and chill until firm. Unmold by dipping into hot water and inverting onto a plate.

Cranberry Cake

serves 15

1 package spice cake mix (chocolate, yellow, or white will also work)
1 bag fresh cranberries

Mix cake according to package directions. Place cranberries in greased 9" x 13" pan and pour cake batter into pan on top of cranberries. Bake according to cake mix directions. Serve with warm Caramel Sauce.

PER SERVING	
Calories:	292
Total Fat:	14g
Cholesterol:	54mg
Sodium:	225mg
Carbs:	41g
Protein:	3g

Caramel Sauce

1 cup brown sugar
1 cup light whipping cream

Combine sugar and cream in saucepan and bring to boil, stirring. Simmer until thickened (soft ball), stirring frequently. Serve with Cranberry Cake.

Saucy *FriChik*® and Asparagus

Cucumber and Tomato Salad

Dinner rolls

Ice cream sandwiches

SABBATH DINNER MENU #32

Contributed by Karin Trees
College Place, Washington

Kristi says: Karin and I have always enjoyed cooking together. Several years ago, after my first trip to Ukraine and a trip she took to Russia, we spent a whole Sunday together cooking Borscht and Pieroshkie while watching the long, black and white version of *Anastasia*.

Karin says: Here are a couple recipes that I have come across over the last few years. I usually go by what I have in the refrigerator to make salad, so it turns out a little different each time. I do like the fact that this is almost a one-course meal and you don't have to do a lot of preparation. It also gives you flexibility to add whatever tidbits you would like. For example, when asparagus isn't in season, I substitute with broccoli.

Saucy FriChik® and Asparagus

serves 6

1/2 pound fresh asparagus spears, halved
1 12.5-ounce can Worthington® FriChik®
1 10.75-ounce can low fat condensed
   cream of mushroom soup, undiluted
1/2 cup light mayonnaise
1 teaspoon lemon juice
1/2 teaspoon curry powder
1 cup grated cheddar cheese

If desired, partially cook asparagus; drain. Place the asparagus in a greased 9-inch square baking dish. Cut *FriChik®* pieces in half and arrange over asparagus. In a bowl, mix soup, mayonnaise, lemon juice, and curry powder. Pour over *FriChik®*, cover, and bake at 350°F for 40 minutes. Sprinkle with cheese. Let stand for 5 minutes. *I like to serve this dish over cooked rice.*

Cucumber Tomato Salad

serves 6

2 large cucumbers, peeled and diced
4 medium tomatoes, diced
Ranch dressing

Toss tomatoes and cucumbers together and add ranch dressing to taste.

Pasta With Fresh Pesto

Bruschetta With Tapenade

Chocolate Raspberry Cheesecake

SABBATH DINNER MENU #33

Contributed by Mindy Rodenberg
Takoma Park, Maryland

Kristi says: Mindy was already an excellent cook when we first became best of friends way back in junior high. On chilly autumn afternoons, you could often find us in her family's kitchen after school, baking Christmas cookies and listening to John Denver records. In fact, she was putting out full-course meals while I was still impressed with myself for adding frozen peas to ramen noodle soup! After all these years, Mindy's kitchen is still one of my favorite places in the world to be.

This menu is nice because you can make the pesto and the bruschetta toast and toppings ahead of time, as well as the cheesecake. On Sabbath, spread the toppings on the toast, pop the bruschetta into the oven, cook the pasta and toss it with the pesto, and lunch is ready!

Pasta With Fresh Pesto

serves 8

4 cups fresh basil, loosely packed
1/4 cup pine nuts
1 large clove garlic, crushed
1/2 cup Parmesan cheese
1/4 cup water

1/3 cup olive oil
1 cup sun-dried tomatoes,
    thinly sliced (optional)
1 pound penne pasta
    or pasta of your choice

PER SERVING	
Calories:	255
Total Fat:	13g
Cholesterol:	36mg
Sodium:	262mg
Carbs:	28g
Protein:	9g

Mix first five ingredients in blender, gradually adding the olive oil until mixture is smooth. Cook pasta and drain. Immediately pour pesto over hot pasta, add sun-dried tomatoes, and stir together. Serve.

Bruschetta

serves 8

1 loaf or 2 baguettes sour dough bread
2 tablespoons olive oil
1 cup chopped tomatoes

1/3 cup thinly sliced green onion
1 tablespoon olive oil
1 teaspoon dried or fresh basil and/or oregano

Slice bread 1/2-inch thick. Brush both sides with olive oil and lightly brown both sides in oven on a cookie sheet. *Slices can be stored at room temperature.* Mix together remaining ingredients and spread on bread. (Tomato mixture will keep, refrigerated, for two days.) *Optional:* Sprinkle with Parmesan cheese and bake at 425°F for about 5 minutes, or until heated through.

A note from Kristi: We recently acquired a tapenade recipe from a family friend, Francis Unger, that adds even more flavor to the Bruschetta (recipe follows).

Tapenade

1 cup pitted olives
2 teaspoons balsamic vinegar
1 teaspoon capers, drained

1 teaspoon olive oil
2 cloves garlic, minced or pressed

Blend all ingredients in food processor or chop very finely. (Tapenade will keep, refrigerated, for two days.) Spread on toast, then top with Bruschetta tomato mixture and a sprinkle of Parmesan cheese. Bake at 425°F for about 5 minutes, or until heated through.

Chocolate Raspberry Cheesecake

serves 8

4 squares of semi-sweet baking chocolate
    or 2/3 cup semi-sweet chocolate chips
1 8-ounce package light cream cheese
1 8-ounce package light whipped topping, thawed
1 8-ounce jar seedless raspberry jam
Chocolate cookie crumb crust (optional)
Fresh raspberries for garnish

PER SERVING	
Calories:	214
Total Fat:	8g
Cholesterol:	13mg
Sodium:	142mg
Carbs:	29g
Protein:	3g

In a microwave-safe bowl, melt chocolate with 1/4 cup water. Use a mixer to blend in cream cheese, 1/2 the raspberry jam, and most of the whipped topping (reserve some for garnish). When mixture is blended consistently, pour into pie plate or chocolate cookie crust. Freeze for four hours or overnight. *If frozen overnight, put in refrigerator to thaw one hour before serving.* Thin the remaining raspberry jam with just enough water so that it can be poured. Drizzle jam over slices of cheesecake and garnish with remaining whipped topping and fresh raspberries.

SABBATH DINNER MENU #34

Contributed by Jeanne Jarnes
Caldwell, Idaho

Jeanne says: You may think this Wellington Surprise looks complicated and difficult to make, but let me assure you, it is not. And it looks and tastes wonderful! Notice that the whole meal is nondairy, even the cheesecake, which is delicious—no one would ever guess that tofu is its main ingredient.

Wellington Surprise

Steamed broccoli
or a favorite green vegetable

Baked potatoes and brown gravy

Summer Tomato Salad

Whole wheat rolls

Chilled Lemon Tofu Cheesecake

Wellington Surprise

serves 12

Pastry:
2 1/2 cups flour
1/2 teaspoon salt
3/4 cup margarine
1 egg yolk
3/4 cup cold water

Filling:
1 pound fresh mushrooms, sliced
2 tablespoons margarine

1/3 pound frozen Worthington® *Prosage®*, crumbled
1 8-ounce package Worthington® *Wham®*, finely diced
1 carrot, diced and cooked
2 green onions, minced, with tops
1 tablespoon minced parsley
1/4 cup dry bread crumbs
1/3 cup water

PASTRY: In a large bowl, combine flour and salt. Cut in margarine until particles resemble fine crumbs. Mix egg yolk with water. Add egg mixture to the flour mixture. Mix lightly with fork until all particles are moistened. Press mixture into a ball. Wrap in waxed paper. Chill for at least 1 hour before rolling out. (Meanwhile, make the filling.)

FILLING: Sauté mushrooms in margarine in a large skillet until tender. Add remaining ingredients. Mix thoroughly but gently. If you are going to bake Wellington right away, cook over medium heat until completely heated. *If you are planning to freeze the Wellington, do not heat filling at this point. Just proceed with rest of instructions and freeze.*

Roll out pastry on a lightly floured board into a rectangle about 12" x 14". Measure and trim sides.

PER SERVING	
Calories:	289
Total Fat:	17g
Cholesterol:	18mg
Sodium:	522mg
Carbs:	25g
Protein:	10g

Place filling down the center of the 14" side of the prepared Wellington pastry, making the Wellington 14" long. Wrap pastry around filling. Moisten pastry edges with water. Seal edges securely down the middle and at both ends. Slightly tuck ends under the loaf after you place it, seam side down, on an ungreased baking sheet.

Cut pieces of the remaining dough and make flowers and leaves or other decorations for the top. Before baking, brush top with a mixture of one egg yolk mixed with one tablespoon water, for a shiny surface when baked. *This makes it beautiful!* Bake at 400°F for 35 to 40 minutes. To serve, place on an oblong serving tray, cut into one-inch slices, and garnish with sprigs of parsley.

Summer Tomato Salad

serves 8

6 ripe medium tomatoes
1 Vidalia (sweet) onion, sliced
2 1/2 tablespoons olive oil
1 tablespoon lemon juice
1 clove garlic, finely chopped

2 tablespoons each chopped fresh
    tarragon, parsley, and basil
1 teaspoon salt
1/4 teaspoon pepper

PER SERVING	
Calories:	69
Total Fat:	5g
Cholesterol:	0mg
Sodium:	301mg
Carbs:	7g
Protein:	1g

Place tomatoes in pan of boiling water for 2 minutes; drain. Rinse with cold water; peel and thinly slice. Place in a bowl with onion slices.

In a small bowl, mix remaining ingredients. Pour over the tomatoes. Let stand at room temperature for 15 minutes. *Since this salad is very juicy, you may want to provide your guests with small individual bowls.*

Chilled Lemon Tofu Cheesecake

serves 8

1 12.3-ounce box silken tofu, extra firm
Juice of one fresh lemon
2 tablespoons honey
1 3.4-ounce package lemon instant pudding
1 prepared graham cracker crumb crust
1 8-ounce container whipped topping

PER SERVING	
Calories:	262
Total Fat:	10g
Cholesterol:	0mg
Sodium:	319mg
Carbs:	39g
Protein:	6g

In a food processor or blender, place tofu, lemon juice, and honey and blend well until smooth. Add lemon pudding mix and blend until mixture becomes smooth again. Place in prepared crust and chill for about 4 hours. Serve with whipped topping.

Fresh Fruit Cheesecake: Prepare fresh fruit (kiwi slices, halved strawberries, orange segments, whole blueberries, etc.) and place in concentric circles on top of cheesecake just before serving.

Fruit Pie Cheesecake: Spread 1 can fruit pie filling over cheesecake before serving.

SABBATH DINNER MENU #35

Contributed by Hope Bushnel
Fresno, California

Jeanne says: Hope has her own catering service. Her business cards read "There's Hope Catering—BIG or small, We do it all!" She is bursting with energy and ideas for good food to serve a crowd! Here's a picnic menu.

Salad in a Basket With
   Raspberry Pineapple Dressing

Angel Hair Pasta Salad

Hot Chicken Casserole

Rolls and butter

Shortbread Brownies

Ginger peach iced tea or
   raspberry lemonade

Salad in a Basket

Line a wicker picnic basket with plastic wrap, then with Romaine or red lettuce leaves. Fill basket with tossed salad made of ingredients such as:

Mixed Greens	Tomatoes, sliced or diced
Torn Romaine lettuce	Carrots, grated or diced
Colored pepper strips	Radishes, sliced
Cucumber, sliced or diced	Red cabbage

Raspberry Pineapple Dressing

makes 2 1/2 cups (20 2-tablespoon servings)

1 cup low-fat mayonnaise
1 8-ounce container low-fat raspberry yogurt
1/2 cup pineapple juice

PER SERVING	
Calories:	36
Total Fat:	1g
Cholesterol:	1mg
Sodium:	120mg
Carbs:	6g
Protein:	<1g

Whip with a wire whisk and place in a decorative container. Place the container in one corner of the basket, surrounded by the tossed salad.

Note: You can use other flavors of yogurt and juice to match flavor: i.e., lemon yogurt and lemon juice. You may need to add a sprinkle of sugar when using lemon or lime.

Angel Hair Pasta Salad

serves 12

1 pound angel hair pasta,
    broken into 2-inch pieces
1/4 cup extra virgin olive oil
8 ounces pesto-flavored feta, crumbled
1 8-ounce container pitted
    Kalamata olives, halved
1 small red pepper, sliced thinly
1 small red onion, sliced thinly

1 carrot, grated
1 English cucumber, cubed
1 cup whole pear tomatoes
1 tablespoon chicken seasoning
    or broth packet
1 small bunch fresh basil, snipped
1 cup cubed Worthington® *Wham*®
2 to 3 cloves garlic, pressed

PER SERVING	
Calories:	*218*
Total Fat:	*13g*
Cholesterol:	*31mg*
Sodium:	*558mg*
Carbs:	*17g*
Protein:	*9g*

Cook pasta as directed on package. Rinse with cold water. Drizzle pasta with olive oil. Toss with other ingredients and serve.

Hot Chicken Salad

serves 12

3 cups Worthington® *FriChik*®, diced
1 10.75-ounce can low-fat condensed
    cream of mushroom soup,
    undiluted
1/2 cup low-fat mayonnaise
1 onion, chopped fine
2 cups cooked brown or white rice
2 cups finely chopped celery
4 teaspoons lemon juice

1 tablespoon chicken-like broth
    or seasoning mix
1 cup sliced toasted almonds
1 4-ounce can sliced water chestnuts
1 2-ounce jar chopped pimiento
1 cup buttered bread crumbs
    or 2 cups crushed corn flakes
    or plain potato chips

PER SERVING	
Calories:	*290*
Total Fat:	*16g*
Cholesterol:	*3mg*
Sodium:	*547mg*
Carbs:	*24g*
Protein:	*12g*

Combine and pour into a lightly sprayed 9" x 13" casserole dish. Bake at 350°F for 45 minutes.

Shortbread Brownies

serves 16

1 cup flour
1/4 cup powdered sugar
1 1/2 sticks margarine or butter, divided
1 cup chocolate chips
3/4 cup sugar
1/2 teaspoon baking powder
2 large eggs or 1/2 cup Morningstar Farms® Scramblers®

PER SERVING

Calories:	207
Total Fat:	13g
Cholesterol:	27mg
Sodium:	120mg
Carbs:	24g
Protein:	2g

Combine flour, powdered sugar, and 1 stick margarine and press into a 9" x 13" baking pan. Bake at 350°F for 20 minutes. Melt chocolate chips and 1/2 stick margarine in microwave. Add remaining ingredients, mix well, and pour over crust. Bake 18 more minutes. Let cool and cut into squares.

SABBATH DINNER MENU #36

Contributed by Del Delker
Thousand Oaks, California

Jackie says: Del prefers to use no dairy products or sugar in her diet. These recipes are some of her favorite and are from the Weimar Institute of Weimar, California. They are used by permission of the Weimar Institute.

Zucchini Spinach Lasagna With
    Cashew Pimiento "Cheese" Sauce

Glazed Beets

Tossed salad

Whole wheat rolls

Kiwi Millet Pudding

Zucchini Spinach Lasagna

serves 10

1 cup chopped onion
1/2 cup chopped green pepper
1 16-ounce can stewed tomatoes, drained
3 cups sliced zucchini or crookneck squash
1 8-ounce can tomato sauce
1 teaspoon salt
1/4 teaspoon sweet basil

1/4 teaspoon oregano
8 to 9 lasagna noodles, cooked
1 cup cooked spinach
   (kale or other greens may be substituted)
Cashew Pimiento "Cheese" Sauce,
   uncooked (recipe follows)

In a large saucepan or frying pan, simmer onion and green pepper in a small amount of water until tender. Add next 6 ingredients and simmer for 20 minutes to make tomato sauce. In a 9" x 13" baking dish, alternate layers of tomato sauce, noodles, spinach, and "Cheese Sauce." Bake at 350°F for 45 minutes.

Cashew Pimiento "Cheese" Sauce

PER SERVING	
Calories:	209
Total Fat:	8g
Cholesterol:	22g
Sodium:	954mg
Carbs:	30g
Protein:	7g

A note from Jackie: I think this Cashew Pimiento "Cheese" Sauce is excellent, quick and easy to prepare, and great tasting.

2 cups warm water
1 cup clean, raw cashews
1 4-ounce jar pimientos
2 tablespoons fresh lemon juice

2 teaspoons salt
1 teaspoon onion powder
1/4 teaspoon garlic powder

Blend cashews with about 1 cup of the water until very smooth. Add remaining water and other ingredients and continue blending until smooth. Pour over the lasagna and bake. *If using as a sauce for vegetables, potatoes, or as a fondue dip, bring to a boil over medium-low heat, stirring constantly, until thickened. Delicious!*

Glazed Beets

serves 8

8 to 10 unpeeled fresh beets
1 cup orange juice
1 tablespoon arrowroot
    or cornstarch to thicken

1/4 teaspoon salt
2 tablespoons lemon juice
1 teaspoon date sugar

PER SERVING	
Calories:	48
Total Fat:	0g
Cholesterol:	0mg
Sodium:	121mg
Carbs:	11g
Protein:	1g

Wash beets. Boil until tender. Slide the skins off when cool. Slice or dice beets. Combine orange juice, arrowroot or cornstarch, and salt. Let simmer until clear and thick, stirring constantly. Remove from heat; add lemon juice and sugar. Stir beets in lightly. *Flavor improves if refrigerated overnight.* Reheat to serve.

Kiwi Millet Pudding

serves 12

2 cups cooked millet, hot and moist
3 cups crushed or chunk pineapple,
    drained (reserve juice)
    and divided
1/2 cup chopped dates
2 tablespoons vanilla
1/4 teaspoon salt
Kiwi or fresh strawberry slices
    or mashed canned apricots
    or other fruit of your choice

Topping:
1 cup pineapple juice (reserved juice)
1 tablespoon cornstarch
Reserved pineapple
Granola or nugget cereal

PER SERVING	
Calories:	209
Total Fat:	1g
Cholesterol:	0mg
Sodium:	82mg
Carbs:	47g
Protein:	3g

Cook millet, using 1 cup millet to 5 cups water. It may take about 30 minutes to cook. *After cooking, measure out 2 cups and eat the remaining for breakfast cereal. Delicious!* In a blender, process cooked millet, 2 cups drained pineapple, dates, vanilla, and salt. Put half the blended millet mixture on bottom of 8-inch square casserole. Layer kiwi or other fruit over the millet. Spread the remaining millet over the fruit. Top with another layer of kiwi or other fruit. Cover with plastic wrap and chill before serving.

TOPPING: In small saucepan, combine pineapple juice with cornstarch. Heat until thickened, stirring constantly. Fold in reserved 1 cup pineapple chunks or other fruit. Pour over the casserole or spoon onto individual servings. Sprinkle with granola or nugget cereal just before serving.

SABBATH DINNER MENU #37

Contributed by Norma-Jean Todorovich
Moorpark, California

Norma-Jean says: The Orange Carrot Gelatin Salad is one of my mother's recipes and always a family Thanksgiving favorite. A friend at Pacific Union College shared the Chum La King recipe with me 20 years ago!

Chum La King

Orange Carrot Gelatin Salad

Green vegetable

Fresh green salad

Fresh or frozen berries
    with whipped topping

Chum La King

serves 10

PER SERVING	
Calories:	*289*
Total Fat:	*16g*
Cholesterol:	*69mg*
Sodium:	*543mg*
Carbs:	*21g*
Protein:	*14g*

1 20-ounce can Loma Linda® *Tender Bits®*
  or 1 12.5-ounce can Worthington® *FriChik®*, drained
1 cup water
1 cup nonfat/skim evaporated milk
2 teaspoons chicken-like broth or seasoning mix
3 eggs, beaten or 3/4 cup Morningstar Farms® *Scramblers®*
1/2 cup light mayonnaise
1/2 cup slivered almonds
1 onion, grated
3 cups chow mein noodles

Mix all ingredients and pour into oiled 9" x 13" baking dish. Bake at 350°F, covered, for 1 hour. *If you reheat the next day, pour a little milk over the top to keep it moist.*

Orange Carrot Gelatin Salad

serves 12

1 6-ounce package orange gelatin
1 6-ounce package lemon gelatin
2 cups hot water
2 cups lemon-lime soda
1 cup grated carrots
1 cup chopped celery
1 cup crushed pineapple, drained
   (reserve juice)

Topping:

1 cup pineapple juice
   (reserved juice + water)
1 egg, slightly beaten or
   1/4 cup Morningstar Farms®
   Scramblers®
1 1/2 cups white sugar
2 tablespoons flour
1 cup whipping cream
   or light whipped topping
1/2 cup grated Cheddar cheese

PER SERVING	
Calories:	256
Total Fat:	3g
Cholesterol:	23mg
Sodium:	119mg
Carbs:	55g
Protein:	4g

Dissolve orange and lemon gelatin in 2 cups hot water. Add soda; let cool. Add carrots, celery, and pineapple. Pour into a 9" x 13" dish. Refrigerate until solid.

TOPPING: Pour pineapple juice and water into a small pan. Add egg. Combine sugar and flour; add to juice and egg. Cook until thickened; cool. Fold in whipping cream or whipped topping. Spread over gelatin salad. Sprinkle grated Cheddar cheese on the top. Refrigerate until ready to serve.

Special K® Loaf

Baked potatoes

Cooked broccoli

Green salad

Garlic french bread

Charles's Favorite Cheesecake

SABBATH DINNER MENU #38

Contributed by Charles and Karla Reel
Meridian, Idaho

Jeanne says: As Treasurer of the Pacific Press Adventist Book Center Retail Division, Charles's office is just around the corner from mine. He can liven up any day with his energetic good humor, and he was one of the first to submit a recipe for this book! Karla is a full-time mom to their two precious children and runs a business out of her home.

Special K® Loaf

serves 10

2 tablespoons margarine or olive oil
1 cup chopped onion
6 eggs or 1 1/2 cups Morningstar Farms®
    Scramblers®
3 teaspoons chicken-like seasoning
    or broth mix

1 packet beef-like seasoning or broth mix
1 cup grated Monterey Jack cheese
4 cups 2% cottage cheese
4 cups Kellogg's® Special K® cereal
1 12.5-ounce can Worthington® FriChik®, diced
1/2 cup 2% milk

In a small frying pan sauté onion in oil. In a large mixing bowl, beat eggs. Combine all ingredients with eggs in the bowl. Pour into a well-oiled 9" x 13" pan; bake at 350°F for 1 hour.

Charles's Favorite Cheesecake

serves 12

1 14-ounce can sweetened
    condensed milk
1 8-ounce package
    low-fat cream cheese, softened

1/3 cup lemon juice
2 cups light whipped topping
1 prepared graham cracker crust
Fresh or canned fruit

In a large mixing bowl, combine sweetened condensed milk, cream cheese, and lemon juice. Mix with hand mixer until smooth. Mix in whipped topping and pour into prepared crust. Refrigerate until ready to serve. Before serving, top with fresh or canned fruit of your choice.

Vicki's Enchiladas

Corn

Cottage cheese

Tossed salad

Favorite drink

Lime gelatin salad made with
    pineapple chunks or lime sherbet

Favorite cookies

SABBATH DINNER MENU #39

Contributed by Vicki Jarnes
Walla Walla, Washington

Jeanne says: Vicki is a no-nonsense cook who knows how to put on a spread for a crowd! When she says "corn," that would be home grown, as would the ingredients for her tossed salad and any other vegetables she might decide to serve along with the meal.

Vicki's Enchiladas

makes 8 9-inch enchiladas (with flour tortillas) or 16 6-inch enchiladas (with corn tortillas)

1 30-ounce can fat-free refried beans
2 cups cooked brown rice
1/2 cup finely diced onion
2 cups shredded cheese, divided (more or less to taste)
8 flour or 16 corn tortillas
1 14-ounce can enchilada sauce
1 14-ounce can tomato sauce

Mix beans, rice, onion, and cheese together, reserving 1 cup of cheese. Spread a large dollop of filling down the middle of your favorite tortillas. Roll up and place in a greased pan. Cut enchiladas in half or thirds (for ease in serving later).

Cover with your favorite enchilada sauce or 1 can enchilada sauce mixed with 1 can tomato sauce. Bake uncovered at 350°F for 20 minutes. Top with remaining cheese and continue baking another 10 minutes or until bubbly.

PER SERVING
Calories: 403
Total Fat: 13g
Cholesterol: 30mg
Sodium: 1118mg
Carbs: 60g
Protein: 18g

Wild Rice Hot Dish

Browned Worthington® FriChik®

Green beans or
   favorite green vegetable

Tossed salad

Herb Bread Rolls

Irene's Cake

SABBATH DINNER MENU #40

Contributed by Dorothy Jarnes
College Place, Washington

Krisi says: Grandma Jarnes has always made sure that no one goes hungry as long as she is around. Growing up, summer vacations were spent at the family cabin in northern Minnesota.

After a day of waterskiing and swimming at the lake, our hungry troop of cousins would climb the path to the cabin and the feast that was always waiting in Grandma's kitchen. If we were lucky, there would even be some Norwegian lefse.

Jeanne says: As any good Minnesotan knows, no potluck would be complete without a good "hot dish" or two. This is one of Mom Jarnes's favorites. Irene's Cake is a moist and delicious recipe from Mom Jarnes's double first cousin, Irene Kelly. Irene's daughter, Lyndel Hieb, is responsible for playing "cupid" and introducing Mom and Dad Jarnes years ago at camp meeting in Anoka, Minnesota.

Wild Rice Hot Dish

serves 8

PER SERVING

Calories:	267
Total Fat:	18g
Cholesterol:	15mg
Sodium:	479mg
Carbs:	20g
Protein:	8g

1 cup wild rice
3 cups water
1 cup canned tomatoes or tomato juice
1 cup grated Colby cheese
1 cup chopped ripe pitted olives
1/2 cup chopped onion
1/3 cup olive oil

1 teaspoon garlic powder
1 4-ounce can mushroom pieces
1 2-ounce jar pimiento
1/2 teaspoon salt
1 1/2 cups boiling water
1/4 cup slivered almonds

Soak wild rice in 3 cups water for 2 1/2 hours or boil 10 minutes; drain. Mix all ingredients together, except almonds. Bake, covered, at 350°F for 2 1/2 hours. Stir several times and add more water as needed. Sprinkle with slivered almonds for last half hour of baking.

Browned Worthington® FriChik®

2 12.5-ounce cans Worthington® FriChik®, halved lengthwise
1 cup flour, seasoned to taste

Coat *FriChik®* with seasoned flour. In a large frying pan, heat a small amount of olive oil and brown both sides of coated *FriChik®*.

Herb Bread Rolls

1 package dry yeast
1/4 cup warm water
3/4 cup milk, scalded
2 tablespoons sugar
2 tablespoons oil
1 1/2 teaspoons salt

3 to 3 1/2 cups sifted flour
2 teaspoons celery or caraway seed
1 teaspoon ground sage
1/2 teaspoon nutmeg
1 egg, beaten or 1/4 cup Morningstar Farms®
    Scramblers®

Dissolve yeast in warm water. Combine scalded milk, sugar, oil, and salt; cool to lukewarm. Add about half the flour and mix well. Add celery or caraway seed, sage, nutmeg, yeast, and egg; beat until smooth. Add remaining flour or enough to make a moderately soft dough. Turn out onto a lightly floured surface; cover and let rest 10 minutes. Knead until smooth and elastic, about 8 minutes. Place in a lightly greased bowl. Cover; let rise until double, about 1 1/2 hours. Punch down; let rest 10 to 15 minutes. Shape into round loaves or rolls and place in greased 8- or 9-inch pie plates or on a baking sheet. Cover and let rise until double. Bake at 400°F for 35 minutes or until done.

Irene's Cake

serves 15

1 package yellow cake mix
1/2 cup Canola oil
4 eggs or 1 cup Morningstar Farms® Scramblers®
1 8-ounce can Mandarin oranges, including juice
3/4 teaspoon vanilla
1 3.4-ounce package instant vanilla pudding mix
1 20-ounce can unsweetened crushed pineapple (with juice)
1 8-ounce carton light whipped topping

PER SERVING

Calories:	321
Total Fat:	14g
Cholesterol:	57mg
Sodium:	337mg
Carbs:	44g
Protein:	4g

In a large mixing bowl, combine cake mix, oil, eggs, and Mandarin oranges. Beat with a hand mixer for two minutes. Place in 9" x 13" casserole dish and bake at 350°F for 25 to 30 minutes. Cool on a wire rack.

FROSTING: In a large mixing bowl, stir together vanilla, pudding mix, and pineapple. Fold in whipped topping. Frost cooled cake and let stand 10 minutes. Refrigerate until ready to serve.

Ratatouille on Rice (or Pasta)

Tossed salad

Corn on the cob

Whole grain bread/rolls

Water with sliced lemon

Strawberry Shortcake

SABBATH DINNER MENU #41

Contributed by Laurie Jarnes Brown
College Place, Washington

Laurie says: Our family is new to the Northwest and the "gardening scene." We have really been enjoying all the fresh produce so abundantly available here in Washington State. This "Ratatouille on Rice" dinner has become one of our summertime favorites. For dessert, I serve a strawberry shortcake recipe I got from my good friend, Nancy Learned. I adapted her recipe to a vegan diet.

Ratatouille on Rice (or Pasta)

serves 10

1/4 cup olive oil
4 garlic cloves, crushed
1 medium onion, chopped
1 medium eggplant, cubed
1 28-ounce can crushed tomatoes
2 bay leaves
1 teaspoon ground basil
1 teaspoon ground marjoram
1/2 teaspoon ground oregano
1 small zucchini, cubed
1 small summer squash, cubed
1 large red pepper, diced

1 large green pepper, diced
3 medium tomatoes, diced
1/2 teaspoon salt (or to taste)
1 15-ounce can tomato sauce
1 tablespoon olive oil
1 12-ounce package garlic and herb tofu, cubed
    or 1 12-ounce can Worthington® FriChik®,
    cubed
2/3 cup fresh parsley, chopped
1 14-ounce can black olives, chopped
8 ounces tofu cheese, shredded

In a large, heavy skillet, heat olive oil. Sauté crushed garlic and onion until onion is translucent. Add eggplant, bay leaves, basil, marjoram, oregano, and crushed tomatoes. Simmer 15 minutes over medium-low heat, stirring occasionally. Add zucchini, summer squash, peppers, tomatoes, salt, and tomato sauce. Stir, then cover and simmer for an additional 10 minutes. In the meantime, cube tofu. Heat 1 tablespoon olive oil in frying pan. Brown tofu cubes. Add tofu and parsley to ratatouille mixture. Continue to simmer (approximately 10 more minutes) until vegetables are tender. Remove bay leaves. Serve over brown basmati rice or pasta. Sprinkle with olives and shredded tofu cheese.

Strawberry Shortcake

serves 9

2 cups flour
3/4 cup sugar
2 1/2 teaspoons baking powder
1 teaspoon salt
1/3 cup oil
1 cup potato (or soy) milk
1 teaspoon vanilla

1 1/2 teaspoons powdered egg
  replacer + 2 tablespoons water
3 pints fresh strawberries, washed,
  hulled, and cut into pieces
1 8-ounce container low fat
  whipped topping

PER SERVING	
Calories:	250
Total Fat:	9g
Cholesterol:	2mg
Sodium:	379mg
Carbs:	39g
Protein:	4g

Mix ingredients together and pour into greased 9-inch square cake pan. Bake 30 to 35 minutes at 350°F until toothpick comes out clean. Cool. Serve with strawberries and non-dairy whipped topping.

Sabbath Dinner Menu #42

Contributed by Aileen Andres Sox and Linda Porter Carlyle
Meridian, Idaho and Medford, Oregon (respectively)

Aileen says: When I was ten or eleven years old, my mother made the best tamale pie. Then the recipe disappeared. Over the years I tried many tamale pie recipes, but never found one I liked as well as the one I remembered from my childhood. Some ten years ago, I was visiting my good friend, Linda Porter Carlyle, and she served her mother's tamale pie recipe. Eureka! It had to be the same recipe. You really do use 3 tablespoons of chili powder. And the coarsely ground corn meal (polenta) is much better than regular corn meal.

Tamale Pie

Green peas

Tossed salad

Pinto or refried beans

Cookies and ice cream

Tamale Pie

serves 10–12

3/4 cup Morningstar Farms® *Scramblers®*
2 cups milk, skim or 1%
1 large onion, chopped
1 can low fat mushroom soup
1 can creamed corn
2 tablespoons oil
2 cloves garlic or equivalent in garlic powder

3 tablespoons chili powder
1 teaspoon salt
2 cups coarsely ground corn meal (polenta)
1 large can diced tomatoes and juice
1 cup grated sharp cheddar
1 large can pitted olives, cut in half

In a large bowl, mix all ingredients together. Spray an 11" x 15" casserole dish with vegetable spray. Pour ingredients into the casserole dish and bake one hour at 350°F. (Tamale Pie can be frozen before baking.)

Sabbath Dinner Menu #43

Contributed by Frances and Joseph Blahovich
Vancouver, Washington

Jackie says: Joseph was pastor of our church in Seattle during the time that all three of our children were married. He is a chef, and he catered every church dinner that was held while he was pastoring there. He and Frances were much loved by their church family. Later, when he and Frances moved to the Takoma Park, Maryland, area, Frances was the favorite teacher of our grandchildren, Kristi and Todd. I know you will enjoy these recipes from Chef Joseph! He has included two desserts: one light and one richer. Your guests can choose.

Holiday Roast

Mashed potatoes

Mock Chicken Gravy

Pineapple Coleslaw

Cauliflower With Cheese

Cranberry Pudding

Baked Apples

Ice cream

Holiday Roast

serves 8

PER SERVING	
Calories:	278
Total Fat:	21g
Cholesterol:	3mg
Sodium:	710mg
Carbs:	15g
Protein:	8g

1 stick margarine
1 large onion, chopped
3 stalks celery, diced
1 12-ounce box herb-seasoned croutons
   or stuffing mix
1 1/2 cups 2% milk or soy milk, warmed
1 8-ounce package (12 slices) Worthington®
   Meatless Smoked Turkey

Sauté onion and celery in margarine until tender. Add to stuffing mix and mix well. Add milk and stir well. Grease one loaf pan. Using a large wooden spoon, press one spoonful of dressing against one end of the pan. Stand a slice of turkey in the pan against the dressing mix. Add another spoonful of dressing to the pan, pressing it against the turkey. Continue alternating dressing and turkey until the pan is full. Cover with aluminum foil. Bake in the middle of a 350°F oven for 35 to 40 minutes.

Mock Chicken Gravy

serves 8

PER SERVING	
Calories:	93
Total Fat:	7g
Cholesterol:	23mg
Sodium:	250mg
Carbs:	5g
Protein:	1g

4 tablespoons olive oil
1 egg
1 onion, chopped
3 to 4 tablespoons flour
1 tablespoon chicken-like broth
   and seasoning mix

Heat oil in a skillet over medium heat. Scramble egg in oil and cook for a few minutes. Add onion and cook until onion is translucent. Add flour and continue cooking for a few minutes. Add water until gravy is desired consistency. Season to taste with chicken-like broth and seasoning mix. Simmer 15 to 20 minutes, stirring often.

Pineapple Coleslaw

serves 6 to 8

3 cups shredded crisp cabbage
1 9-ounce can (or 1 cup) pineapple tidbits, drained
1/2 cup low-fat mayonnaise

Mix all ingredients well. *For variety you can add 1 cup diced unpeeled apple, 1 cup mini marshmallows, and/or 1/2 cup chopped celery.*

PER SERVING	
Calories:	65
Total Fat:	4g
Cholesterol:	5mg
Sodium:	76mg
Carbs:	7g
Protein:	1g

Cauliflower With Cheese

serves 8

1 head cauliflower
1/2 cup shredded cheese

Wash cauliflower and steam, whole, for two minutes. Set the whole head of cauliflower on a microwave-safe dish and cover with shredded cheese. Microwave for 2 minutes. Garnish with parsley sprigs. To serve, cut into wedges at the table.

PER SERVING	
Calories:	32
Total Fat:	2g
Cholesterol:	7mg
Sodium:	48mg
Carbs:	1g
Protein:	2g

Cranberry Pudding

serves 8 to 10

2 cups fresh cranberries, washed
1/2 cup light molasses
2 teaspoons soda + 1/2 cup water
1 1/2 cups flour
Sprinkle of salt

Sauce:
1 cup sugar
1/2 cup butter
1/2 cup whipping cream
1/4 to 1/2 teaspoon vanilla

PER SERVING	
Calories:	268
Total Fat:	12g
Cholesterol:	34mg
Sodium:	87mg
Carbs:	40g
Protein:	2g

Combine in the order given. Spray the top of a double boiler with cooking spray. Fill lower half of double boiler with two inches of water. Pour the cranberry mixture into the top of the double boiler. Steam on low heat for 2 1/2 hours.

Mix SAUCE ingredients in a saucepan. Simmer over medium heat until butter is melted. To serve, pour warm sauce over individual slices of pudding.

Baked Apples

serves 4

4 apples, washed
1 cup Red Hots (cinnamon candies)

Core out center but don't cut through bottom of each apple; fill with Red Hots. Place apples in a glass casserole dish. Cover Red Hots with water. Microwave for 5 minutes or until apples are tender; serve topped with ice cream.

SABBATH DINNER MENU #44

Contributed by Bonnie Herbel
Caldwell, Idaho

Bonnie says: These *Redi-Burger®* "Meatballs" are so quick and easy to prepare. They are not fried so this recipe contains no added oil.

Redi-Burger® "Meatballs"

Mashed Red Potatoes

Green beans or squash

Tossed green salad

Orange-pineapple gelatin salad

Dinner rolls

Chocolate Cream Dessert

Redi-Burger® "Meatballs"

serves 10

PER SERVING

Calories:	234
Total Fat:	6
Cholesterol:	102mg
Sodium:	1043mg
Carbs:	23g
Protein:	22g

Meatballs:

1 28-ounce can low-fat Loma Linda® Redi-Burger®

1 cup Italian seasoned breadcrumbs

8 ounces nonfat cream cheese

5 eggs

Gravy:

2 cans condensed low-fat cream of mushroom soup

1 cup nonfat sour cream

1/2 teaspoon au jus mix (French dip style) or beef-like broth and seasoning mix

1 teaspoon Kitchen Bouquet Browning & Seasoning Sauce

1 cup 2% milk

Mix MEATBALLS ingredients together well. Form into 1 1/2-inch balls and place in rows in a greased 9" x 13" casserole dish. Bake at 350°F for 30 minutes. Meanwhile, combine GRAVY ingredients; mix well. Remove meatballs from oven and cover with gravy. Return to oven and bake for another 15 minutes.

Mashed Red Potatoes

serves 10–12

5 pounds new red potatoes

2 teaspoons salt (or to taste)

1/4 cup butter or margarine, divided

1 1/2 cups 2% milk

PER SERVING

Calories:	198
Total Fat:	5g
Cholesterol:	2mg
Sodium:	426mg
Carbs:	36g
Protein:	5g

Cut potatoes into 1-inch squares (do not peel) and place in a 5-quart saucepan. Sprinkle with salt and fill pan with just enough water to cover potatoes. Place pan on stove burner and bring to a boil. When at a rolling boil, turn down to a simmer, leaving lid on. Simmer for 20 minutes. Test the potatoes with a fork to see if they are done. Drain the water off the potatoes. Using a potato masher, mash the potatoes. Add 2 tablespoons margarine or butter and 2/3 to 1 cup of milk (making sure the potatoes are not too dry). Mix well. Pour into serving dish and dot with 1 tablespoon margarine or butter.

Chocolate Cream Dessert

serves 15

1 1/2 packages chocolate sandwich cookies, crushed (do not remove filling)
2 to 4 tablespoons butter, melted
1/2 gallon vanilla ice cream, softened
1 8-ounce container low-fat whipped topping

PER SERVING	
Calories:	280
Total Fat:	16g
Cholesterol:	39mg
Sodium:	200mg
Carbs:	31g
Protein:	3g

Mix butter with approximately 2/3 of the cookie crumbs and press into a 9" x 13" glass dish that has been sprayed with cooking spray. Bake at 350°F for 10 to 15 minutes. Cool. Mix together ice cream, whipped topping, and remaining cookie crumbs. Pour over crust. Freeze for at least 1 hour before serving. Cut into 3-inch squares and serve. *You can decorate with crushed or whole chocolate sandwich cookies.*

WORTHINGTON® FOOD INDEX